Bermuda Shorts

Bermuda Shorts

James J. Patterson

Alan Squire Publishing
Bethesda, Maryland

"The Conjecture Chamber" first appeared in *Stress City: A Big Book of Fiction by 51 DC Guys* (Paycock Press, 2008); "The International Aeronautical Sanitation Administration," "Gordo, God & Gandhi," and "Something Out of Nothing" appeared in a slightly altered form in *WordWrights Magazine*. "Gabbing with O'Reilly," "The Myth of the Casual Fan, "The Mayor of 417," "The Nearest Thing to Perfection," and "I Study the Crowds" appeared in *SportsFan Magazine*. "I Am a 9-10er" and "Walter Johnson: Baseball's Big Train" first appeared on SportsFanMagazine.com. "The Conversation We Are Born Into" appeared on www.JamesJPatterson.com.

Bermuda Shorts is published by Alan Squire Publishing in association with Left Coast Writers and The Sante Fe Writers Project.

ISBN: 978-0-9826251-2-5

Cover painting by Rose Solari and Sandra Bracken.
Jacket design by Randy Stanard, DeWitt Designs, www.dewittdesigns.com.
Back cover photo by Rose Solari.
Inside jacket photo by Zak Patterson.
Copy editing and interior design by Nita Congress.
Printed by Proforma Mactec Solutions, Oakland, CA.

Visit www.JamesJPatterson.com.

First edition
Ordo Vagorum

For Rose Solari, Al Johnson, and Joanna Biggar

Chaos is the score upon which reality is written. —*Henry Miller*

The writer's role is to *menace* the public's conscience. —*Rod Serling*

I will have no man in my boat who is not afraid of a whale! —*Starbuck*

Contents

Foreword

Greg Wyshynski

"What is he looking at?"

It was a question lingering on the brain in nearly every editorial meeting for the late, great *SportsFan Magazine*—a D.C.-based periodical that combined staunch sports fan advocacy with sublimely ridiculous sports coverage, symbolized by a logo that literally gave the reader a thumbs-in-the-ears, fingers-in-the-air raspberry.

The editorial staffers would sit in chairs of varying degrees of comfort, meeting agendas in our hands and earnest attempts to follow them in our hearts. James J. Patterson would be seated at the right hand of the Sonny Jurgensen photograph on the back wall of his cluttered office, behind an ancient desk whose surface was stacked with notions and whose drawers were jammed with reveries.

The meeting would go as planned: Story concepts thrown at the wall, cover stories suggested and then spiked, malleable deadlines established. Jimmy would participate as warranted, but he already had the next edition laid out in his mind before the meeting even began—something that allowed him time to pursue other interests as we yammered away.

"Seriously, what is he looking at?"

It could have been a computer screen filled with the vital political news of the day, or a just-discovered website that labeled particular genera of flatulence.

It could have been an essay on God's place in the modern world, or liner notes to *Blood on the Tracks*. (Jimmy would argue they're one and the same.)

He could have been glancing out the window, wondering how much longer a suburban Maryland town would need a vacuum cleaner repair shop, or checking out the business end of a blonde scurrying inside the line of the crosswalk on her lunch break.

What was he looking at? Life. Love. Liberty. Libations. The lighthearted and the ludicrous, the lewd and the lamentable. He'd witnessed so much, consumed so much, that his mind couldn't help but race to the next search for life's fragile truths, or the next brief clarification of its mysteries.

His findings and philosophies, collected in these works, echo the words his band heard from countless radio program directors during their time making subversive politically incorrect (but surprisingly catchy) ditties: "There's no category for you guys."

This collection blissfully defies classification, which is a tribute to its impact and its scope. Vivid characters from his past teach him, guide him, frighten him, and entertain him, while doing the same for us. It's an expedition through temples of the mind to temples of worship, blurring the boundaries of both when parrying with a friend's curious intellect about concepts of faith.

He's got faith in his own concepts, too. "Beauticide," or the unwavering urge for humans to destroy things that are beautiful. "The Conjecture Chamber," where dread and insecurities cloud rational thought after the loss of a compatriot. Becoming the unelected "mayor" of an upper deck section in a sports arena. Hurling all the toxic and destructive materials man creates into the smoldering center of our universe, turning the sun into a kind of cosmic incinerator. An idealistic world where, he writes, "boredom and cynicism are not mainstream expressions of cultural futility."

Bermuda Shorts is where nostalgia, art, humor, and perennial skepticism combine in a search for meaning, where philosophy can be found kneeling in front of a haunted crucifix, amongst the vibrating stands in a temple of sports, or in a prolonged tête-à-tête over a bottle of Wild Turkey 101 on a road trip.

It's about life: the whimsy of it, the losses that come with it, and the dutiful journey through it.

It's what James J. Patterson has been looking at; it's a vision that deserves to be shared.

Greg Wyshynski is the editor of Puck Daddy, *a Yahoo! Sports hockey blog, and the author of* Glow Pucks & 10-Cent Beer: The 101 Worst Ideas in Sports History. *He used to sit in meetings staring at Jimmy Patterson as features editor with* SportsFan Magazine.

Acknowledgments

I would like to thank the staff, teachers, and members of The Writer's Center in Bethesda, Maryland, and my incredible good fortune to have stumbled upon such a place when I did.

> *I think Literature—a new, superb, democratic literature—is to be the medicine and lever, and (with Art) the chief influence in modern civilization.* —Walt Whitman, 1888

Few know this better than the following:

R. D. Baker, Joanna Biggar, Rose Solari, Alan S. Johnson, Alan Sonneman, Greg Wyshynski, Pete Sweigard, Cynthia Matsakis, Meinrad Craighead, Grace Cavalieri, Linda Watanabee McFerrin, Lowry McFerrin, Dan Patton, Rita Ricketts, Willy DeLeeuw, Sunil Freeman, Charley Pick, Andrew Gifford, Nita Congress, Richard Peabody, Randy Stanard, Zak Patterson,

Quinn O'Connell, Jr., Mary Von Drehle, Jack & Dorothy, Mancheenee (John F. Patterson), Murray Freeburn, and Loraine Vahey.

James J. Patterson
Bethesda, Maryland
February 2010

The Reluctant Scholar

The Lovesick Lake

Chubby Blewett made cedar-strip boats by hand. In a year he could make two, but their future owners had to want them bad enough to call him often, write him letters, and otherwise display a genuine appreciation of his efforts. It also helped to go down to the old boathouse next to his cottage by the lake and keep him company while he worked. Everyone on the lake owned at least one, and, properly cared for, they would last a long long time.

At dawn each morning during the summer, I would stir in my cozy down-filled bed at the steady drone of Chubby's boat as it passed our island at the north end of Lovesick Lake. He would cut his engine, drop anchor, and cast his nets for the big chubs or chubby minnows that made his bait and tackle shop famous. As silence returned to the lake, I would drift back to sleep until the swallows that nested in the eaves outside my window began their giddy morning ruckus.

The story goes that a young Ojibwa girl, upon hearing of the death of her lover in a far-away war, threw herself from the open dam at the southern end of the lake. He returned unharmed and, when he learned of his love's fate, he chose to perish in the same swirling rapids at Burleigh Falls. So the lake was named Lovesick. But there is a deeper history there as well.

In 1896 an English couple, John and Emily Marshall, purchased a land grant from Queen Victoria for a five-acre island in the Trent Canal System in Central Ontario, Canada. Emily, then thirty-four years old, and her husband named the island Clovelly after their honeymoon retreat in England. Her husband owned a peanut farm in Africa and when he retired, he shipped from his African estate a giant stone he called "Elephant Rock" and placed it under the arm of his favorite oak on Clovelly Island. The Marshalls employed many of the Ojibwas from the nearby Curve Lake Native Reserve as day laborers to build gardens and trim the hedges that formed a lane from the main house to the boathouses at the island's rocky southern end. These laborers built elegant wooden archways through the forest on the north side that led to Emily's favorite swimming place. Pine branches were fashioned into comfortable benches where one could rest and appreciate a view. Gazebos looked out over the sunrise and sunset points. They built a putting green. They also filled the woodhouse, maintained the sawdust in the icehouse, and saw that the kerosene lamps were filled and the wicks were fresh. They emptied the honey buckets from the two outhouses into a deep hole at a far mossy end of the island.

Emily busied herself writing poetry and painting costumes on ceramic elves that everywhere peeked out from behind rocks and trees. Emily enjoyed painting elves, fairies, and angels on the walls inside the house as well, and when she tired of her creations she simply nailed another black plaster-board to the pine walls and began her work anew. She nailed new carpet over old in the same manner.

Mr. Marshall died on January 1, 1929, and Emily had his ashes encased in stone and placed at the foot of Elephant Rock.

I first saw Clovelly from the seat of one of Chubby Blewett's boats. My father told my sister and me to wait while he went up to the big white house. Three very old ladies wearing flower print dresses and large straw sunhats sat fanning themselves on the shaded porch.

"'I would will this island to the Boy Scouts before I would think of selling it to a man who took a drink!'" my father quoted Emily later that day over a Canadian Club and Coke. That winter, not an hour after signing Queen Victoria's deed over to my father, Emily Marshall died. It was her ninety-sixth birthday. Her nieces had her cremated and, when the spring thaw came to Lovesick Lake, they sprinkled her ashes over Clovelly Island.

For the next ten summers, I filled the kerosene lamps and saw that the wicks were fresh. We cooked our meals on the iron woodstove in the kitchen, picked wild choke cherries for making jam, kept the outhouses neat, and cleaned the porcelain chamber pots that went beneath the beds at night. We fought the giant spiders that lived in the rotting wood and, piece by piece, we burned the decaying remnants of Emily Marshall's century in the bedroom stoves and the giant living room fireplace. We were convinced we could hear her cry on those nights when the wind and the lake were calm and the only sound as we went to sleep was her sighing hiss from the fire.

Twice a week Mr. Spencely brought giant blocks of ice that he carried up from the dock with big frightening tongs and buried in the sawdust in the icehouse. We would chip off hunks with an ice pick for the icebox in the kitchen. The Ojibwas asked for permission to harvest the rice that grew wild in the water behind the island, and sold it back to us cheap along with big bags of delicious juicy frogs' legs skinned and ready to cook.

When I was ten years old, my father commissioned old Chubby Blewett to build for me one of his prized sixteen-foot cedar-strip boats. It was the greatest gift I was ever given and easily the grandest prize I will ever know. The bottom and inside floorboards were painted red to my personal specification. I called the boat Charley after a boy I had known in school who had moved away before we had a chance to become friends.

My older sister and younger brother and myself were each allowed to invite a friend up for the summer, or portions of it. This involved a delicate recruiting process for each of us, using my mother's charming diplomacy as a last resort. Our friends were always very curious about where we went to spend our summers, and it wasn't without some lament that we said goodbye at the end of each school year, knowing that when we returned all would be different, old friends would have forgotten us, changed, moved on. Kids change a lot over a summer. Those who decided to brave the trek north with us had to know how to swim, first and foremost, had to get tetanus shots, and had to have some resistance to poison ivy. They also had to be down with the concept of how to Make Your Own Fun, and understand that chores aren't merely annoying responsibilities assigned to build character, but essential if you wanted to eat, have water to drink, or keep warm. Some who came lasted a week and had to go home. We would snicker to ourselves knowingly as we waved goodbye. Others loved it and, like us, never wanted to leave.

We would explore the nearby uninhabited islands, go fishing, skinny dipping, and sneak out at night to play boat tag with the teenagers around the lake, amazing them with our intimate knowledge of the rocks that lay treacherously beneath its more shallow surfaces.

One friend of mine from back home who took to the place like a brother was Willy. He was a big strong kid, on the hefty side, just perfect for weighing down the bow of my boat. We would hide behind forest islands and ambush the giant cabin cruisers that came down the main channel and go boat-surfing in their wake. Willy would giggle hysterically as he got soaked. We would guide the Sunday morning fishermen out of the weeds, out of the rocks, out of the rain. We would guide the drunks on the lake home at night, knowing they would never remember how they got there until the next time we guided them home. Some would think that they were being boarded by freebooters as we pulled up alongside at full speed in the dark, but after a quick paddle fight they'd surrender to reason.

Once, while following Willy across stepping stones through the rapids below the open dam at Burleigh Falls, a rock slipped out from under my foot and I was swept off by the fast-flowing current. "Swim! Swim hard!" Willy yelled as he followed hurriedly along on foot across the rocks. When he saw that my struggles couldn't overcome the strong flowing water, he skipped ahead, and, just feet from the next steep waterfall, he reached in and plucked me out. We stood quietly, overlooking the falls at the jagged rocks below for several minutes. I would have gone right over. There's not a chance I would have survived.

Late at night, silhouetted against the bright Canadian moon, drunken Dr. Howell, with his beagle standing on the bow of his boat, would cruise up and down the lake singing at the top of his lungs, "Jesus keeps his money in the Bank of Montreal!" to the tune of "The Battle Hymn of the Republic." One day, I stopped him on the mainland docks to ask him how the rest of the song went and he looked at me as though I was crazy.

One summer, my mother got all of the "bad boys"— mostly native kids who hung around the government docks— together and organized a fast-pitch softball team she called the Burleigh Falls Swingers. They won every game. The only way I could get on base was to stick my leg out and let the ball hit me. But life was hard for the local kids, and by the time I was an adult all but two were dead—even the lovely Barbara Brown, my age, who would call me from the reservation and flirt with me and coax me to come and meet her under the bridge at Burleigh Falls. My mother said that if I encouraged her, the locals would beat her for hanging out with a white boy. I stayed away. The following winter, I overheard my father take the phone message that she had been killed in a car wreck. She had been decapitated.

By the summer of 1968, the charm of nineteenth century living had worn off. We were the last family on the lake to give in to modernization. Plumbing, electric lights, and a telephone were novel but we never could bring ourselves to get a TV.

You see, we lived, during the school year, in the suburbs of Washington, D.C., but we grew up on Clovelly.

Clovelly was where my father told my mother he wanted a divorce. They never got one. She never set foot on the island again.

As I grew older and life swept me up in its own fast, relentless currents, I would travel whenever I could to Clovelly to vacation alone, or retreat there to heal and reinvent myself. As I evolved into a writer, a musician, and whatever else I became, it was at those times between careers when Clovelly would call to me. In my dreams, I would fly effortlessly, always at night in the dark, with the stars in the heavens as my guide, circling the island three times upon each arrival and each departure.

Once alone on the island, I would slowly syncopate my routine with the patterns of the sun and moon, to the rhythms of the tides and the big rotating sky, the birds—loons, herons, and gulls—and the raccoons, flying squirrels, beaver, and chipmonks. Dogs love to swim, and there were several around the lake who liked to huff and puff their way through the water to come and visit me and frolic together on Clovelly Island. Sometimes when I was on the mainland for supplies, one of these hounds would approach me for a familiar pat on the nose and a scratch behind the ears. His master would say something like, "He don't usually like strangers," to which I would reply, "Well, I might be strange, but I'm not a stranger."

Coming up the lake at night when there was no moon and the waters were rough would scare visitors from the city half out of their wits, which was nothing compared to the fright they were in for once they confronted themselves alone on Clovelly Island. Many turned back. It astonished me to learn that some people have never known real quiet, have never had a chance to extinguish the noises and distractions of modern life long enough to listen—really listen—to their inner self, their true self, in conversation with the world. I felt sorry for them and tried in vain to make them understand. If they didn't—well, what can you do?

I didn't notice at first and can't tell for certain which summer the wild rice that grew in the shallows between islands disappeared along with the lily pads and the giant frogs that bellowed so hilariously at night. Perhaps it was the same summer that aluminum and fiberglass boats began to outnumber old Chubby's cedar-strips on the lake. Once I got older, my cedar-strip boat didn't seem so long and lean. The five-and-a-half-horsepower engine at the back was slow, but it only served to remind me not to be in such a hurry: important things are to be seen and experienced all around.

In 1979, my second business failed. I threw everything I owned into the back of my Boston Cream Cutlass and left Washington, D.C., for Lovesick Lake. An artist friend of mine, Charles Young, or Cy, as we knew him, who was in similar straights, joined me for the first few weeks. Willy joined us too for a brief time. I would write all day and burn my creations in the fireplace at night—offering, if you will, the sacrifice of my efforts as good medicine to the spirits that permeate Clovelly Island. Besides, the stuff wasn't any good.

Cy painted big canvases of clouds and water and rocks. Willy busied himself doing chores, and helped himself to any of the dozens of books from our makeshift library. Willy helped us rig a water hose over a picture window, and Cy photographed the distorted lake country landscape through the moving water, took portraits of some of us, and painted from those bizarre and distorted images. The effect was startling, with floating eyeballs, swirling coutryside, and remnants of reality.

At night we sat in my cedar-strip boat, drank Gold Tassel Rye or Labatt's Blue, and watched the sun fall and the giant galaxy emerge within our well-oiled reach. We turned slowly beneath the triangles of Shedir and Epsilon. We were Shedirians, Epsilonians, emigrants yearning to return home. In August, the northern lights hummed a strange and dissonant refrain. We still maintain that we could hear those lights, though experts disagree. One night, we were tracking a satellite through the firmament when suddenly it made a perfect right-angle turn and disappeared into purple blue-blackness. No one has yet explained that phenomenon satisfactorily.

When we got bored, we would drive to the nearby town to meet girls or invite friends from the local campsite by the locks for a weekend of Murder in the Dark. You put pieces of paper in a hat. One says Detective, one says Murderer, all others say Victim. Whoever draws Detective is sequestered in a well-lit room with something to read. The person who draws the Murderer card keeps that information secret. Then the lights are turned out. The murderer then gets to kill as many victims as possible (usually by simply whispering "you're dead" in the dark) until someone stumbles over a body and must call the Detective in. The Detective then interviews the survivors and makes a determination as to who the killer is. It's a fun parlor game if you have a big house. On a dark and forested island, it becomes something else again.

I complained to the local boys at the campsite on the mainland once about an Esso gasoline sign—certainly illegal—that had been erected on a publicly owned island about a half-mile across the lake from Clovelly. The government maintains these uninhabited islands to preserve the natural beauty of the area, so there's a ban against this kind of commercialization. And this beast was three stories tall, made of wood, with the circular metallic Esso logo in the middle. Very few boats had traveled the main channel that year, and my beef was that they were really only advertising to one man—me!

So, late one night there was a knock at the back door on Clovelly, and twenty crazed Canadian teenagers raised beers in the air and shouted, "We're going for the sign!" I could hear them hammering and sawing, their curses and laughter echoing across the water all night, and just before dawn they towed their prize back and set it up against the woodshed on Clovelly Island. Luckily, I had enough beer to reward them all. We took a group picture. We then chopped up the wood and buried it under pine needles where it waited for the fire. We laid the giant Esso oval across the bow of my cedar-strip boat and, at the deepest part of the lake, we broke a bottle of Blue over it and sang, "Oh Canada!" as we watched it glide into the depths. No one ever missed it.

When Charles and Willy left—Cy for California, Willy for the oil patch in Montana—I stayed on, and, for the next two years, I listened to the trees. The squirrels would come to me when there was trouble in the nests. I talked to the woodchucks, racoons, beaver, and birds. I lay naked on the gravestone beneath Elephant Rock and read John Keats out loud. "A thing of beauty is a joy forever!" I sang to the loons. I read hundreds of books. When people in town would stop me on the street and ask me if I was okay, I had to think about it.

One day, back in Washington, my mother phoned and gleefully informed me that the island had been sold. They didn't need the money. I was furious at not being given a chance to buy it myself. I called my father to ask what in the world had happened, but his normal thunder was missing. His best friend had just dropped dead while pushing a lawnmower. I took him to the funeral. We never mentioned Clovelly.

I doubt we ever will.

Sculpture Isn't…

Down the road from the local community college is a dingy little Italian restaurant. The cockroaches and sleazy leering waiters are the reason that most of their business is take-out. But the food is okay. The wine is excellent. The privacy is indispensable. I like to come in mid-afternoon with a book of poems and my journal, when the restaurant is changing over from lunch to dinner, when there are few if any patrons. I can relax. I can think.

Eating and drinking and relaxing and thinking. It is a wonderfully mammalian process for slipping between worlds.

Over my first glass of wine, I open a book of poems by Lawrence Ferlinghetti and at once I am struck by a seemingly insignificant line. On another day it might have gone unnoticed, sitting there amid dizzying line breaks, but today it boldly steps forward like one of Voltaire's mighty aphorisms, just puzzling enough to force me to pull together the disparate strings that dangle about my random thoughts into something useful.

"Sculpture isn't for young men."

It occurs to me, as I read the line again, that I have only recently entered middle age. I can still pass as a young man. I've even been carded for alcohol in the last year or so. But I am no longer young.

When I was fifteen, my parents, fearing that my sister and I were becoming too concerned with frivolous suburban pursuits, sent us to spend the summer in Florence, Italy. We ran out of our summer's allotment of cash in just a couple of weeks. My sister fell in with a burly bearded sculptor named Arturo Demonica. I found a job in the flea market during the day, hawking leather goods to English-speaking tourists. At night I would drink up my pay at a renovated wine cellar turned bar—a tourist trap, really—situated below street level, owned by those same vendors for whom I worked during the day. In the afternoons, during siesta, I would take a sandwich and a bottle of water to the nearby museum and have lunch at the foot of Michelangelo's *David*.

I entered the museum from a damp narrow street, flashed a museum pass to the dozy guard, and down a long echoey corridor, there he was. Tall, beautiful, perfect in every way. Except one.

I would sit on the floor in the circular rotunda, eat my sandwich, and, as I contemplated that calm, unself-conscious naked man gazing out above the heads of his admirers toward the street, I would think, no, something here isn't right.

Tourists, students, older couples, young women would stroll in and approach the statue with deference. Most would

be immediately embarrassed by the beauty of his total naked-
ness, and recover long enough to express some admiration
and wonder at the fact that it is, after all, a piece of stone and
not a real live naked man. I, on the other hand, would be willing to say that it *is* a real naked man, just not flesh and bone. I
sat there and gave it a kind of life. And everyone who entered
that room did too. It draws a spark from each observer, until
it appears to breathe in the reflected essences projected upon
it.

Now, decades later, sitting in a seedy restaurant outside
of Washington, D.C, the capital of another empire, I can give
voice to my misgivings over that statue. You, sir—with your
flaccid stare and your leg bent in casual haughty observance,
with your weak aristocratic mouth and delicate wrists, your
hip pushing forward and rounded haunch, standing there
without a stitch of clothing on—you may be a lot of things,
my friend, but one thing I'm sure of, you aren't slaying anyone
today, or any other day, pal. Even though your sculpting is perfect right down to the print on the toe that juts out from the
pedestal at eye-level height, or the wisp of hair like dissipating
steam from the cauldron of your tempestuous and youthful
thoughts. No, you're no killer, nor savior, nor everyman chosen by fate. You're just a lonesome naked man. A boy, really.
Vulnerable in every way. Like any perfect thing would be in a
rough-hewn wilderness. With a slingshot over your shoulder
to accentuate your defenselessness.

Sculpture isn't for young men.

Most definitely I agree. Explaining why is difficult.

I am thinking now of older men I have met, admired, or
known. Folk singer Dave Van Ronk, poet Will Inman, my college philosophy teacher, the writer Henry Miller, who did his

important work after the age of forty, Ferlinghetti himself, me ten to fifteen years from now, the fellow who has entered the restaurant and taken a table a few feet away.

My Caesar salad arrives and I order another wine.

Dave Van Ronk's belly sags over his 1970s-style corduroy bell-bottoms. It's the late 1980s and his Scandinavian hat, the vest over a tattered shirt, his yellow tobacco-stained fingernails, all contrast with his well-trimmed beard and ruddy, boyish face. Is music another vice for him? I wonder. Does degeneration, as in the degeneration of his lungs, his cigarette cough, mean that much—has he affected the voice of the characters about whom he sings for so long that it is, by now, his own? He is partially famous because Bob Dylan copped his version of "House of the Rising Sun" for Dylan's first album. It was a naughty thing to do. But in the long run, it may have helped gain Van Ronk many new listeners. It was how I heard of him.

A group of us have been summoned to an all-hit radio station in Manhattan to perform funny songs live on an April Fool's comedy show. Being an all-hit station, they wouldn't be caught dead playing any of our "independent" records. We know, and they know, the wrath that would descend upon them, should they ever report playing anything other than major label product. Sure, they can have us play live, but no recordings. So we must travel from near and far to play songs live that they could otherwise just spin from our CDs. It's an insult to be an independent artist and get invited here. More people will hear this show than will probably pay to see any one of us in a given year. No one turns them down. Dave Van Ronk, in particular, is past concerning himself with the trifling vicissitudes of the business of his craft. Van Ronk's girlfriend, or wife, stands just taller than his waist; half his age, she kisses his hand as it rests on his tummy as he waits to go on. Peculiar, intimate, beat.

Will Inman was my poetry teacher in college. Hemingway-esque in appearance, he had heard that I loved poetry and writing, so he sought me out and invited me into his honors poetry class. This was 1970. I was eighteen and a struggling student trying to keep my grade point average high enough so as not to lose my draft deferment. He gave everybody an automatic A. His gesture was important to me. More than that, he treated us with respect, and worked hard to ensure that we earned his favor.

My philosophy teacher, meanwhile, whose name I have forgotten, began his course with a stunning observation. "Sixty years from right now, every person in this room will be dead. In the face of that, we must judge how seriously to take the subjects to be explored here."

I was stupefied. Intrigued. In total agreement. Then, however, I interpreted his remark to mean, not seriously at all; now I would say, seriously enough.

I was walking down a hall one day and heard a strange noise coming from an empty classroom. When I looked in, I saw him, sprawled across a desk in the throes of a horrible asthma attack. His face was brilliant red. Spittle streamed from his mouth as he struggled for air. I offered to get help but he waved me on. I thought about the incident a lot. I dropped his class. My encounter with him in his private agony only served to convince me that I couldn't take his class. I feared this guy would break my heart. I saw the flawed philosopher in myself and felt that love, women, and the endless search for meaning would have to proceed without a guide.

There is something tragic, fleeting, self-destructive about these men of poetry and song. Relishing in their mortality, they seem to convey a sense of satisfaction in their slow degeneration, as if the example of their passing lends legitimacy to their expressions of it. All as beautiful as David when they started out, now, as men, they know true things. These can be read in the lines of their faces, seen in the humor hidden behind their eyes, felt in the coarseness of their once-soft hands, heard in the gravel of their voices, driven by hearts almost weary.

Ten years removed from college, I found myself alone on Clovelly Island, after business failures had sent me packing to a faraway place to collect myself and reinvent my reasons for existing. From a box of books I had brought with me I picked out a copy of Henry Miller's *Tropic of Cancer* and read those first fateful pages: "I have no resources, no money, no hopes. I am the happiest man alive. A year ago, six months ago, I thought that I was an artist. I no longer think about it. I am." And I realized that my whole life had to start over again. As it had before and would, no doubt, have to later on.

Sculpture isn't for young men.

A fine piece of work I was. Young men are for sculpting, by women, life, and the time of man into which they were so unexpectedly born.

Huidekoper

"**G**oddamnit Goldilocks, wake up!"
My head is pounding and my mouth is dry. No.
My head is not pounding. It is the walls that are pounding. Someone is outside pounding on the glass, pounding on the door. *Make them stop!* Whoever it is must be looking in the big bay window just above the bed. I force open an eye and frantically check to the right and left. Luckily, I'm alone.

I'm not alone. Someone is screaming. "Goldilocks! Open the goddamn door!" I roll awkwardly off the mattress that lies on the floor and climb to my feet. My hair, normally past my shoulders in long tumbling curls, is sticking out in all directions. My face is a sagging pile of goo. I can't afford an air conditioner and the ancient electrical system that services this basement apartment/office couldn't handle one anyway. It is ninety-five degrees inside. It is eight o'clock in the morning and already I'm dripping sweat. I throw open the door and there he is. A retiree from Patton's Third Army, complete with brushcut hair and white overalls. He's holding a paintbrush in one hand. In the other he holds a filterless cigarette between two sawed-off stubs that once were fingers. Three fingers from his right hand and two from his left were burned off when his machine gun overheated during a battle long ago. He's looking at me with utter disgust.

"Jesus Christ, Goldilocks. Would you please put on some pants!"

I look down and yes, it's true, I'm completely naked.

Lewis, the house painter, follows me through the office to the laundry room in the back of the basement. As I pull on a pair of cut-offs, he opens the fridge and helps himself to a beer. He brings me one too. He knows I can't afford to waste a thing so pops it himself before handing it to me, thus making sure I won't put it back. That's got to be an old army trick, I'm certain.

"Why is everyone I know trying to kill me?" I ask.

Lewis likes to tell stories about tank battles back in The War. World War II. I don't know if I can begin my day with one. Mercifully, he is coughing so hard that he hasn't heard my casual reference to murder; therefore, a verbal connection between our mutual mortality and Lewis's bloody past is not made. He has recently had a lung removed and is too busy destroying the other one to pay much attention. We'll do the tank battles later. Maybe over lunch.

I leave Lewis to his painting and head upstairs for a shower. The guy I share the house with has left for work, so the place is mine. I take the beer into the shower with me, and set it on the handhold above the soap dish. I stand under the cold water and by the time it reaches my ankles it is warm.

Another day has begun on Huidekoper.

Huidekoper Place, pronounced Hi´-dee-cope-er, is a cozy little cul-de-sac nestled into the hilly backstreets of Georgetown in Washington, D.C. It is where I landed after a series of post-college traffic accidents persuaded me to give up driving a truck in the middle of the night for *The Washington Post*. It became, for a select group of us, a laboratory for Experiments In Adult Living, sagaciously carried out between the years 1976 and 1979. One of my greatest moments there was killing a fast-moving cockroach with a wet sponge from about eight feet away while doing the dishes.

I'm in the shower when Sam arrives. Samantha Pennington is known for her steadfast dependability in a sea of insecurity, misconception, and dread. When I get back downstairs, the mattress is gone. The two desks that face each other under matching bay windows are meticulously organized. She is making calls. For me, another script treatment waits. She corrects my work from last night while she cuts a deal on the phone. She is a wonder. A cum laude lurking behind bewitching blue eyes and natural cornsilk blonde hair. We are not lovers, although my female friends remain unconvinced, suspicious, and quietly resentful. I rather enjoy that.

Sam and I have been good friends since high school and have served as part-time confidants and accomplices through the misadventures of those years. We have agreed that we are much too valuable to one another as friends and business partners to muck it up by getting physical. We've seen what happens to those who take on that challenge. It never lasts long, and it never ends well. As a business partner, she keeps me organized and focused, plus her social charm and maniacal enthusiasms have won us many allies I could never have solicited on my own. As her friend, I am able to penetrate the minds and intentions of her male consorts, and she in turn is able to lure many unsuspecting females to my lair. I'm the only one who calls her Sam. She prefers the nickname Penny. We are quite a team.

Our primary business is taking classic stories from literature and turning them into radio dramas that we sell as complete episodes or in serials. Unlike the scratchy dramas of yesteryear, we generate most of our own sound effects, taking advantage of the new era in FM radio's broadcasting quality and the consequent boom in home audio equipment, aiming our product at the home audio enthusiast. Our current subject is Sherlock Holmes. We have, through the British Embassy, met some actors and been given an introduction to the Baker Street Irregulars, an exclusive worldwide organization of Holmes aficionados who have been passing the word about our project. We've also raided the campus of Catholic University, famous for its acting school, for cheap talent.

At exactly noon, the upstairs doorbell rings. It is Miss Blake from down the street. Miss Blake goes by her maiden name, as she has outlived her third husband, a Supreme Court justice, by thirty years, and has very little personal affiliation with so distant a past. It is she who has, by virtue of her seniority among the other widows on the block, taken on Lewis as one of her many philanthropic projects. Every summer she chooses a house on the street that she will argue needs painting. These are two-story brick townhouses, and so the outside painting consists mainly of window frames, eaves, and doors. She does not ask their occupants' approval or even warn them about the person they are so unexpectedly about to spend the season with. Lewis is therefore kept occupied during the warm season, as she calls it, so he can live comfortably year round. It is up to us to find the money to pay him. She has brought him lunch. I open the sack and there is a sandwich, an apple, and two cold Budweisers.

"Lewis likes beer," she whispers clandestinely, "hope you don't mind." Him drinking on the job, she means.

"Well," I answer a little apprehensively.

"Oh come on!" she scolds, "He's a veteran, you know." On her way back down the street, she calls the squirrels out of the trees one at a time for a little treat. She knows them all by name, talks to them in clicks and whistles, and they answer her call. I'll be damned if I don't understand what she's saying to them. "Mama's baby want a grape?" "Does little darlin' like raisins?" "Would little sweetheart have some nuts?" I close the door and pop one of the beers on my way up to the roof to find Lewis. Sam grabs the apple, pours some fresh drinking water into a mason jar, and joins us.

"I was in love once," Lewis reminisces over deviled ham. "It was just after the war. We lived together until I discovered she was a lesbian. Honest, I didn't care. I loved her anyway. After you've killed a lot of people you don't care much about that sort of thing. You just like people for who or whatever they are, but her girlfriend wouldn't have me. A shame, though, because I kinda liked her too."

As a sideline to our business producing audio masterpieces, we manage a country music band. Jimmy Carter is president and anyone with a guitar and a buckskin jacket can make damn good money here in the Capital of the Empire playing for the transplants from Georgia and the South. Rural Virginia and Maryland have a country music following. The band has a huge urban, suburban, and rural fan base. The best of most worlds. The players are really just a bunch of hippies from New York and the D.C. area playing what they call kick-ass country music. At the height of the disco era, and before the Punks and the New Wavers take over, outlaw country has an authenticity that gives it a brief alternative appeal. One band member is a Berklee College of Music grad, and his complicated arrangements, along with the music theory and history he imparts to the others, make every performance something to look forward to.

On two different occasions, aggressive, overachieving males will leave high-paying media jobs to join our company. We advise them not to do it. They could be of much greater help to us by staying at their jobs, tossing us their table scraps, and spreading the word of our efforts to their contemporaries. We are desperate for the help and expertise they could bring, but we know the pitfalls of being self-employed. They don't.

From the safe distance provided by company expense accounts and big salaries, these men have been spoiled by union-negotiated health care and the prestige of having a big-time corporate appellation attached to their names. They will take no direction, no suggestions, brook no demands or criticism. They are driven by a false confidence, a form of hubris, stemming from the mistaken impression that they are indispensable. For them, the romantic status of being independent, of replacing the corporate master with a mastery of one's own, has a seductive appeal. And once set free, they will be incapable of being subservient to their new bosses—us.

Soon, a kind of horror sets in. The empty blotter at the beginning of each day, when rent and meals hang in the balance, becomes a baffling scourge. Their illusions about who and what they are can't possibly hold up out here, in our world, where we are anonymous, unprotected, and only as good as the last buck we made—or didn't make. Day after day these guys sit frozen, incapable of forming a conjecture on how to proceed, how to prioritize; their old cronies stop taking their calls, and "cold calling" is anethema to them.

Had they looked more closely, they might have noticed that they were about to join a team where everyone, from the musicians, actors, soundmen, freelance photographers, visual artists, and graphic designers, to our little cabal of business managers, are all about twenty pounds underweight. We are great fun to hang out with, true, but we count our collective purses before going to a bar or out to eat. We hang out together because there's nowhere else to go. We don't leave our jobs at the office because we can't afford to. Meals at the end of the month are thin, and skipped often. This is our life. These guys weren't ready for that, and they just wouldn't listen.

Of course, they failed—ruinously, to themselves—and devastated our little enterprise.

One, Gordo Sinclair, left a big-time editing job with network news to help get the band we manage a record deal. It was then we learned from executives in Nashville, Macon, and Atlanta that the music industry works in counterintuitive ways. The industry does demographic studies on what they think they can sell, then they put the acts together, or find something already up and running in New York or LA to fill the need. They certainly don't just grab some act that's damn good with a big following and promote them. If they did that, the cocaine addicts in New York and LA skyscrapers would be forced to get out on the hustings, research and develop, and put in some overtime following up, to justify their existence.

Gordo became addicted to coke himself, stole my girl, stole the band out from under us, failed at both, and wound up on what used to be called Skid Row. No one was sorry for him.

Chuck Herrington left a big-time radio station in a major market to help sell our radio plays. He fell in love with a succession of bimbos, proposed to one, took us for what cash we had, and never spoke to us again. Gordo rehabilitated as a nice guy, became a schoolteacher, and returned one day to say he was sorry. Chuck, we are sure, rehabilitated demonically, roaming his community looking for anything remotely bohemian, and then devoted himself to passing legislation to get it, and people like us, outlawed. We labeled them both MIA— Missing In Action.

William Zachary Harper, Willy, my housemate, has a foot in both worlds. He is my best friend from grade school. Between the band, the radio plays, and his day job, he won't get a full night's sleep in four years. He is the youngest vice president a local bank has ever had. Under the mentoring guidance of his boss, a banking visionary, he is helping to create an international division which means gathering the embassy accounts from their competitors under one executive services plan that is quite compelling. Once the accounts are signed up, it becomes Willy's job to lend them money. The sky's the limit! The bank encourages him, because they feel a loan guaranteed by a government empowered to print money can't go bad. He tells of giving away the store to all who come asking. Meanwhile, the same bank demands collateral in excess of two hundred percent of what we are borrowing for our little business.

Consequently, it is left to Sam and I, with Willy's help on the side, to pull the load. It is really only a matter of time before the load pulls us down. A window of opportunity is open, but the resources to take advantage of it are running out. This we know. We play the game against time, against ourselves. The canyon floor seems so very far below and the breeze on the way down is lovely.

In the meantime, Willy arrives home after work and over his first glass of Dewar's reviews our efforts of the day. He listens to our triumphs and near misses, and we listen to his exploits at the bank. We are news junkies, rock'n'roll addicts, philosophy majors, and literary mavens. Artistically we pile genres on top of one another—country music, jazz, nineteenth century sound effects, Irish ballads, Chicago blues, classic radio bits from yesteryear—as easily as we play with radical political concepts. My current hero is Alexander Pope, and somehow we fold his playful sincerity into the rendering of our endeavors in a kind of myth-making that is so very easy to fall in and out of. In following the edicts adopted from the great poet, we "love our pain," we "change what we can," and we "laugh, laugh, laugh at the rest!" But we do it while imitating the speech patterns of Basil Rathbone, the greatest Sherlock Holmes of all.

Willy has roots in the great Dakota Badlands which gives him a Rooseveltian sort of aggressive optimism, so he assumes a rough and tumble approach to everything from doing the dishes, to scrubbing the bathrooms, to working with clients, to drinking and driving.

At night, after dinner, we pile into Willy's Jeep, the one that he parks in front of the Stodgy Old Bank every day, like a horse in front of a saloon, and hit whatever bar the band is playing in. His Jeep, a ragtop CJ-7 he has named Tatonka, the Lakota name for buffalo, suits him perfectly. Sam and Sylvia, an actress buddy from our recording sessions, love to tag along for the fun of picking up strays.

With Willy at the wheel, we tackle the night. We tackle our foes. We tell ourselves we are on a crusade from which there is no turning back. Sometimes we believe it.

Willy is a workaholic, but on those nights when he is able to break free and join us with the band at a club, we always manage to save him a seat or a table front and center. After two drinks, he falls sound asleep, as a hundred decibles roar. Alvo, the gregarious band leader, standing center stage directly above Willy's table, will in the millisecond between beats cry into the microphone, "C'mon Willy, wake up!"

On hot summer nights, Willy stows the doors of the Jeep behind the tire rack on the back. One night, I yell at him to slow down while rounding a curve. We are nearing a woman's house where I hope to spend the night. When he doesn't respond, I look up to see that he is no longer behind the wheel. Sam and Sylvia, riding in the back, grab me in time to keep me in the vehicle as we go up on two wheels, but we lost Willy out the door. Seat belts? What are they?

"How'd you stop the Jeep?" he asks incredulously when he comes running up a few moments later.

In answer, I point to the trees, the lawns, torn-down fences, and decimated suburban flower gardens in our path. The Jeep is halfway up a big old tree trunk.

The next morning I will wake to his familiar voice outside my girlfriend's open window. We can see Willy Harper. He is standing there in a most serious three-piece suit and cowboy boots, coolly explaining to the police and a consortium of neighborhood residents, in the one-hundred-degree heat, that he can't possibly be charged with reckless driving. He wasn't even in the vehicle at the time of the accident. He assures them that he can produce witnesses. Damned if they don't let him go.

"I want to write his speeches when he runs for president," I say.

Across the street from us on Huidekoper lives The Mad Painter. Charles Winston Young is a tall, dark, and handsome Minnesotan, who has rejected his parents' generation's stultifying uptight Germanic religious mores to become an uptight recluse artist in, of all places, Washington, D.C. His friends call him Cy. He has replaced Jesus with Art, ritual with discipline. No one and nothing is good enough for him. For some reason, he has adopted us and become our self-appointed conscience, a sort of cultural quality control expert. His greatest fear is the corruption of his aesthetic. And the most potentially dangerous heretics and apostates, the possible usurpers of his Pristine Chapel, are, of course, his friends. The gauntlet is always thrown. I find this educational, and his challenges refreshing. Others find him a huge pain in the ass.

Cy shares his house with two stunning females. This has earned him entry to our domain, without knocking, at any hour of the day or night. He usually chooses the dinner hour to exercise his option. But he always thinks to include one or both of his housemates. One is a dirty blonde gymnast named Natalia, the other is a petite, raven-haired, ivory-skinned half-Spanish, half-Russian, who has moved to Huidekoper directly from a convent in Germany. The nunnery wasn't for her, and for that we are all grateful.

Cy, The Mad Painter, likes to sit up late in my basement office and drink Canadian whiskey and argue with Willy, Sam, and me, and whoever else has wandered in, about art, literature, and politics. The funny part about arguing with Willy and Cy is that we argue while at the same time agreeing on almost every salient point. Screaming our heads off, yet in near total agreement, each of us shouts his next point, forming layers of rhetoric like we're from a secret society of Jesuit novitiates gone horribly wrong.

Cy takes us with him to gallery openings and leads us around to shows he thinks are important. He's a big man and he picks fights with curators, patrons, waiters, and other artists over points of art appreciation. He is on a personal campaign to shame the government, chambers of commerce, and the various corporate headquarters in the region into supporting the Arts by adorning their lobbies and outer areas with original art. At this he is very successful and an inspiration to those cynics among us who think ivory towers unscaleable. He's mad, of course, in both senses of the word, angry and insane. But who isn't? It's a great escape for me to stroll across the street and pace about his studio as he paints the day away, standing or squatting with his nose just inches from a very large canvas, his mind churning over the inefficiencies in whatever argument has been offered as the current fare. Hanging around writers suits him. In fact, I think it's healthy for artists of different disciplines to inter-mingle. There's no professional jealousy to alter our appreciation of one another. Visual artists are always looking for an outsider with a reliable eye, a different perspective. And besides, writers always have something good to read lying about.

One night while The Mad Painter, Willy, Sam, and I are in a harangue in my basement apartment, there's a tap on the window. A handsome thirty-something sandy-haired guy is standing there in the darkness above the back alley, wearing a lumberjack shirt, boots, and jeans. He introduces himself and says that an ex spook we all know told him we had a couch in the basement here he could borrow for the night. Washington, D.C., is a town full of spooks. Spooks, spies, security analysts, agents, and their administrators—the bleeding town and the surrounding environs are crawling with them. Aside from the fifteen hundred private security forces in D.C., there are twenty-two federal security agencies, populated by thousands of spooks and their enablers. And contrary to what you might think, these people, like the rest of us, like to get drunk and bitch (and boast) about their jobs. There's a lot of ex spooks, spies, security analysts, agents and their ex administrators and enablers as well. They *really* like to bitch. The Huidekoper Team runs into them all the time. We are three blocks down from the new Russian Embassy compound at the top of the hill. We are five blocks from the vice president's mansion in the old Naval Observatory at the top of Embassy Row. And every other person at the local bars appears unusually quiet, or foreign, and mildly amused when our troop comes stumbling in, arguing politics or working through the myriad of social issues that beguile and vex us from one minute to the next.

So we tell this guy okay, but just for a night.

He stays a couple of weeks.

"Do you know you're being watched?"

Come to think of it, we have noticed Ford sedans idling out front from our place and down to the dead end of the street. One or two straight-looking guys are always inside, smoking cigs and watching everything.

"Yes, but who are they?"

"It's hard to say. We have so many agreements with other countries that let us spy and break the law in their countries, there's naturally reciprocity among international intelligence communities. It could be anyone."

Foreign cars, more of a rarity back then, make an appearance too. Parking is a premium in this old neighborhood, and these guys, thinking perhaps they are invisible, stick out like sore thumbs to anyone looking for a space.

Our phones are clicking and beeping and hissing too. "Israeli intelligence," Willy speculates. He has been cornering the market in international banking with an emphasis on Middle Eastern—meaning Arab—countries.

"Well, as long as they stay in their cars and don't call their friends everything should be fine. So you'll stay off the phone and out of sight?"

"Sure."

At the prospect of being bugged we are sanguine. Someone listening in would learn all about band bookings, audio production problems, script rewrites, mailing lists, and romance.

One night, he returned and gave us a real fright. He had taken a pair of scissors to his hair, cutting his sandy locks into random shards of uneven lengths. Scarier still, his right pupil had exploded. Where there was earlier in the day a normal round black dot, there was now an uneven square, like a little black box with the bottom ripped out. His speech was hesitant and jittery and he wasn't making much sense. Something had happened and he couldn't tell us what.

The next day the guy was gone. And, thankfully, he never came back.

Roaming the side streets in post-Watergate D.C. has us seeing shadows in every parking garage, and looking for signals from balconies, and hidden in newspapers. We begin to see everything through this fantastic lens. Even poor old Lewis starts to take on a sinister, conspiratorial air.

On a night when the band was playing at a nightclub on M Street in Georgetown to a packed house, I was standing by the soundboard in the back watching the show. The band was roaring through a pro set. The whole gang was there and having the time of their lives. And watching them it came to me. It was over, and I was the only one aware of it. I knew what Gordo was about to pull, I knew Chuck was a failure. I knew my girl was going to jump ship. I knew that the band members were still enthralled with Gordo's bombastic swagger, and that the power play he was about to initiate would prevail, but that ultimately, he would not. I leaned back against a wooden column like a man stunned, and sipped my beer. The smoke, the music, the people I loved, this moment, would stay with me as a funereal bookmark to this chapter of my life. They were all so happy, but by their own misshapen loyalties, they were all so doomed.

The next day, when Willy learned of Gordo's defection, he banged his fist on the dinner table so hard he broke his wrist.

On another day, at the bank, he arranged for a loan of several million dollars to a company in Spain he would later find out was a shell organization for a consortium of arms merchants who used the money to buy weapons to kill innocent people in South America. It put him off his international banking career and sent his conscience spiraling off into deep dark space. Willy sold everything and took off in his Jeep to become a roughneck throwing chain in the American oil patch out West, dropped the name Willy and became Zak. Only Thomas Merton's pale philosophy and Native American mysticism could follow and retrieve him. Everyone has to find their own secret cure for what ails them, I suppose.

A white station wagon came for Miss Blake on a hot spring afternoon. She cried as she blew goodbye kisses to the squirrels. Sam moved to a group house full of really sweet people, married a nice guy, and then came down with an incurable arthritis. Lewis met a predictable end. The Mad Painter split for California, where he still paints giant canvases and argues with everyone. I split for Canada in a used car full of books, a typewriter, a guitar, lots of blank paper, and embraced my new status as a man of no importance.

Winston Churchill once said that "A success is someone who can go from failure to failure without losing enthusiasm."

Long after I turned the key on Huidekoper, I remain its devotee.

That Was Then,
This Is The Pheromones

"There is no use knowing what is to be; for it is wretched to be tormented to no purpose." —Montaigne quoting Cicero, c. 1588

"Look at it this way, if we don't go, we'll never regret not staying home." —Alvis Pheromone, c. 1988

This is exactly the type of remark for which my partner is nearly famous. I am about to tell him so. Angrily. He is three hours late and I could tell by the sound of the van as it chugged down the street that it hasn't been fixed. Because he's so late, we'll now have to hump it down the highway late into the night in order to make it to the upper Midwest all the way from Washington, D.C., in time to make our sound check tomorrow night. He's been gulping down coffee, which means he'll take the first shift and drive until it wears off and he gets sleepy. Then he'll give me the wheel. There will be no coffee available then, it will be dark, and, as soon as he hits the passenger seat, he'll go right to sleep. He'll feel safe, oddly enough, because he knows I've been in eight major car accidents and survived each one relatively unharmed. Consequently, whatever the hazard or circumstances, I don't fall asleep at the wheel. I'm good in a crisis. I look at him with genuine disgust verging on loathing.

His face is haggard and there are scary-looking bags under his eyes. His newborn has colic. He works like a slave at home, logs hours by the dozen in our office booking gigs, and is a relentless picture of stamina and stick-to-it-iveness on the road. He's broke again. I tell myself, *Leave him alone.*

I trudge back into the house for some goodbyes. Three days before a road trip such as this, my wife stops talking to me altogether. She barely acknowledges my presence. I know I'm being punished in advance for leaving her alone to take care of our child. She can't be blamed for sulking. She has never seen, or smelled, the inside of a Motel 6 or a Super 8. She would never voluntarily put herself in a situation where a nuked steak-and-cheese sub and burned four-hour-old coffee were her only available forms of sustenance.

She thinks college kids still read good books.

"Hey Dad?" my four-year-old calls me back after refusing a goodbye kiss, "don't forget to take this with ya!" and then punches me as hard as he can, right in the balls.

The bridge from Superior, Wisconsin, to Duluth, Minnesota, opens a tall and strange vista. It reaches high above the Port

of Duluth with only highway construction blocks, Jersey bar-
riers, guarding the edge. At dusk, deep blues and grays mingle
in air so cold that it cannot hold a mist. Steam rises from the
ice below and dissipates swiftly, blown to nothingness by huge
random winds that roll unimpeded over the frozen plains of
Lake Superior. I want to stop here, hundreds of feet above the
ice, and listen. I want to hear the ice bend and groan. I want
to hear the quiet echo of it on the hill across the water where
eerie lights glimmer. I want the wind to slap my face and freeze
the tears that smear my temples. But there is no time for spontaneous mystical delights.

The van is garish and loud. The engine screams. The
heater is on full blast and we are still freezing. The equipment in the back rattles. The mike stands clang when we go
over a bump. The fact that we could hit the brakes and both
be harpooned is the least of our worries. Our stage clothes
are hung neatly down each wall, and the hangers clatter
against double-plated steel as the van sways from side to side.
Curtain rods squeak. I swear sometimes it all sounds like a
group of old men wheezing and laughing at us through spent
tubercular lungs.

Thank god for books on tape. On this trip we have something new from Ray Bradbury and Martin Balsam reading
Henry Miller's *Tropic of Cancer*. Ten days into the trip we've
got *Cancer* memorized. Al starts to take on a Milleresque
appearance. Balsam, Miller, and Alvis Pheromone are all from
Brooklyn, and Al can translate the subtleties of Brooklynese
literally and figuratively. We buy all our clothes at thrift shops
as we move around the country, and the current trend is
1940s–'50s pleated slacks, long coats, and bowling shirts. Al
has found an old gray fedora. In his long coat, hat, and baggy

slacks, he looks like an unemployed university professor from between the wars. What I look like is anybody's guess.

The two of us perform at community colleges and remote campuses of state universities, bars, and coffee houses where most East or West Coast entertainers would never dream of going. Like goliards of the thirteenth century, we roll quietly into town, set up, spend an evening lampooning the social, political, and religious structures of our day, the local poobahs, and the universal constabulary, then quietly leave before anyone can do or say anything about it. Marketing geniuses that we are, we have chosen a name for our act that no one can spell, pronounce, or understand.

We use pseudonyms.

The kids don't know what to make of us. We are not going to be on David Letterman and don't aspire to be. Because of that, we are, to them, an anomaly. We are independent and therefore completely free to say what we please. The worst that can happen is not to get invited back, and getting invited back isn't bloody likely anyway. A third of these audiences are charmed. A third are ambivalent. Another third are incensed. The college kids are accustomed to being drowned out by the music they listen to and by the messages that bombard them from every direction. I am older than many of their teachers, but look like I might actually be one of their own. At a table between sets, a young man asks what my favorite rock band is.

"Midnight Oil," I reply.

"How old are you?" he wants to know.

"Twenty-seven," I answer, deceiving him by ten years for his own good. "Why do you want to know?"

"Because they're my favorite band too. I just wanted to know how old I'll be when I stop liking them."

Weird. Somehow a notion has crept into the psyches of these young people that at a certain age, like pod people, they will wake up one morning changed, that the things they believe and enjoy will somehow become strange to them, that they will, in effect, turn on themselves and betray their inner truths.

Perhaps they will.

Another night I am chatting with some kids after a show. One of them is a philosophy major. He tells me he is fearful about his future, that everyone—his parents, his friends, even some of his teachers—tells him he has made a catastrophic choice of curriculum.

"I never met a history, English, or philosophy major who didn't go out and get a job," I tell him. "You're going to be fine. Just remember this, you don't go to school to get a job, you go to school to learn how to think. Believe me, the jobs will come."

He tells me that no one has ever spoken to him like that before.

At least five times on this trip, faculty advisors will apologize for the low attention and comprehension values of their students. "Whose fault is that?" I will ask.

Young male intellectuals crave some form of initiation. We carry a bottle of Wild Turkey 101 with us at all times for that very purpose. Al passes it around after a show and makes them recite passages from Miller. Their devotion is true.

In Bimidgi, Minnesota, the entire ROTC comes to our show. Twenty years ago they would have been laughed off campus, shunned, and given no pussy. Now they hate us. They sit in the front row and after every song they stand in unison, pump their pretend shotguns, and blow us away. We usually play sixteen songs each set. That night, we play two sets. By about the tenth song, we drop the original material from the show, and finish doing just covers. The show goes dead. We get paid and get out of Dodge.

Some nights we play four sets, or sixty-four songs. Al will laugh that the more sets we are required to play, the less we get paid. The really high-paying gigs only want one set.

In our career, we'll never have less than fifteen hundred college and public radio stations playing our CDs every day. Most times, the number of stations playing our stuff is closer to three thousand, but, remarkably, we don't chart on the boards that rate such airplay because "there's no category for you guys." So a major label band with a mere three hundred stations is Number One. When we began this adventure, we also had three hundred commercial open-format stations playing us in heavy rotation. By the time our second album came out, that number was down to twelve; the rest had either been bought out, changed format, or been driven out of business. By our third album, two commercial "alt" stations remained; by our fourth CD, there were none. The clampdown on stations playing independent labels was complete. To survive, we had to call individual DJ's around the country with specialty shows merely to get a spin.

At the noncollege venues—bars, folk clubs, concert halls, alumni gatherings, conventions—a similar paradigm to the love us/hate us/don't know what to make of us routine is in effect. Since we are very good at what we do, we make it look easy. And because it looks easy, we get this kind of comment:

"So you guys just read the paper and write this stuff. Anyone can do that, right?"

"Well sure, go ahead," I suggest, as though in full agreement. "I tell you what, we'll be back in four months. You write some songs and we'll let you get up between shows and you can play them. You can't beat an offer like that."

"But I don't play the guitar, I can't sing."

"Ah, I see."

Others condemn us for being subjective liberal partisans in our gags and more serious material. "How can you call it entertainment if you have an opinion?" is a frequent query. "Why don't you give both sides a fair shake?" they scold.

"Well, I tell you what," I answer. "You spend half your life learning to play an instrument, devote yourself to studying all you can about the genre you want to perform, then quit your job and put all your time, money, and effort into finding venues to play in, risk your health, your family's well-being, live hand to mouth never knowing if it's all going to come crashing down and put you out on the street as soon as your schedule runs out, no pension, no health care. Do all that for the paltry sum they charged you to get in here tonight, and then you tell me how objective you're going to be once you step up to that microphone."

But here's the one I love the most: "So, what's your *real* job?"

During the height of the Reagan Conservative Era, we find that audiences, perhaps a full third of them, had lost—or I should say more accurately, had never cultivated—the ability to suspend disbelief. These are people who interpret the Bible literally, but not the Constitution.

In radio and print interviews, we call it "theater-phobia," a scary mob-directed need to have whatever is put before them be as unchallenging, unthreatening, and black and white as possible. The audience members can't tell they are being set up for a punch line, and so can't get the punch line. From the stage, we see in them a frightening refusal to invest themselves in the entertainment they have paid to see. They are either completely for us, completely against us, or complacent to the point of sitting there stupefied.

My partner is tall, dark, and traditionally handsome. I'm short and fair with long curly hair, and pretty damn good looking, as well. As a gag, we introduce ourselves as brothers.

"Twins, can't ya tell?"

"Same father, different mothers."

"We were joined at the nose at birth," I love to riff on Al's prominent proboscis.

One reviewer, in print, actually asks, un-ironically, "Why would two musicians, who are clearly unrelated, try to pawn themselves off as brothers?"

We are constantly researching, attempting to define what is going on. Why the disconnection? It's hard not to blame it on what we see all around us—a general deconstruction of culture by a conservative/religious movement attempting to discredit all that stands outside the narrow confines of its own illusions of reality. In the van, I'm reading Edward Gibbon's *The History of the Decline and Fall of the Roman Empire.* I think he understands what we're going through.

"The decline of genius was soon followed by the corruption of taste," he writes. Certainly, one result of the devaluation of cultural genius, by society at large, is *theater-phobia.*

◈

The starry-eyed college kids have a less ego-driven, less hubris-laden query. "What's it like driving all over the country playing music?"

"It's fabulous. I can't imagine doing anything else," we say. "They're putting us up in the old unused dorm hall at the other end of campus tonight. The heat isn't too good but we get to eat in the cafeteria later for free. You can't beat that!"

Every once in a while, when we read a hostile audience correctly, or when the news on the street meshes perfectly with the message from the stage, we strike a chord with them that we can actually feel resonating through the teeming, roiling mass before us. That enthusiasm carries an amperage that is life sustaining to us as much as or more than the money we are or are not making. It gets us through the bad nights and long treks through hazardous and unfriendly territories. That response is an audience's spontaneous collective and unconscious way of returning the favor. We can turn them, given half a chance.

Artisans from other disciplines ask us, over beverages late at night, "Is what you guys do *art*?" And the honest answer is, "Sometimes."

An artist, or, I should say, good work, can change the recipient's life for the better. When that happens, you know it. We are fortunate that we are actually in the room to witness the transformation. Sometimes you move an entire audience, and they leave the building changed from when they entered just hours before. You don't get paid for that, it only saves your soul.

◈

Often it takes until four in the morning to pack up our gear and return to the motel. You don't get twenty-four hours when you rent a hotel room, no matter what the class of the joint. Work all night and check in at four in the morning and they still want you out as soon as possible. Tell the poor slob behind the bulletproof glass, or the stodgy-faced uniformed person behind the marble countertop that you demand a "late check-out" and no matter what his or her response, the maids will be making loud noises in the hallways at seven a.m., and start banging on the door at eight. At eight thirty they use their key and enter and reenter the room every twenty minutes. You can bark at them, you can call downstairs, you can lay there buns-up naked. Some get the message, some don't. Either way, your ass is out by eleven.

On our current trip, we will do sixteen gigs in thirteen days, then leave the van in Minneapolis and fly to Seattle, rent a car, and do another dozen shows in the Pacific Northwest. We will nearly get killed by a deer. We will travel through deforested mountains and visit volcanoes and nuclear waste dumps. We will then fly back to Minneapolis, reacquire the van, and gig our way through upstate New York, where we will nearly get killed by another deer, and then down through Pennsylvania working our way home. Al chatters quietly to himself during his shifts behind the wheel. By now, our wives are barely speaking to us. The kids won't come to the phone.

In the van, I wrap my woolen overcoat about me like a baby blanket. I wear the darkest sunglasses I can find.

◈

Bombs or No Bombs, Business as Usual

Gordo, God & Gandhi

My friend Gordon wants to talk about God. He has called me from work, and over the course of his rambling dissertation on the state of things in his life at present, wonders aloud why "nobody wants to talk about God anymore." By "nobody," I assume he means his peers. He wonders why it is not a topic of conversation among his intimate friends. Real people. In all the years we've known each other, why haven't he and I discussed it, he asks. By "anymore," I presume he means that God, and more specifically, the existence of God and the very essence of faith, was once a central concern of his and his acquaintances.

Gordon majored in religious studies at a Southern university, got a summer job at a TV station, and has been working in television ever since. Twenty years have somehow elapsed. Keeping that in mind and by way of warming up to the subject, I point out that there is certainly a lot of *public* talk about

God going on. Professional proselytizers, like angry little cartoon urchins banging away on kitchen implements thinking they are making music, are ubiquitous, and would be amusing except that they are intolerant of Gordon and I, and they want to rule the world.

Their opposite numbers in the secular spiritual movement, if that's what it's called, are filling bookstore shelves with manifestos—in some cases articulating a charming sort of ersatz-Buddhism, in others a refreshing and, I feel necessary, environmental revisionism—that sees *the divine* in everything. Gordon, I would have thought, is a prime candidate for this group. He is personally warm and generous, sincere, educated, and concerned about the quality of his inner life. But he is oddly oblivious to the entire alternative spiritual genre, perhaps because he clings to an inflexible Biblical definition of God, and perhaps, too, because his mainstream training in television has taught him to be suspicious of anything that can't be pigeonholed. So he has avoided this highly self-involved industry for what it is, self-involved. He isn't really in need of a support group, doesn't really feel victimized, except, that is, by everything, so emotional and spiritual "healing" is not high up on his hierarchy of needs.

As for me, being a bit of a hell-raiser, I don't care. Because some sort of authentic spiritual affirmation is missing, or is wanting definition in the culture at large, it's a party I'm willing to crash. But for those who are skeptical of alternative spiritual movements and who feel that traditional religious organizations are missing their mark, there is a void.

As I tell Gordo to put his antennae up and his nose to the breeze, I can't help but think that he is ripe for some Robert Bly, Margot Adler, or Joseph Campbell to come along and help him initiate the epiphany he so clearly yearns for. Gordo brushes me off, says he wants to get past all that, whatever *that* is. Gordo has faith and trust in our friendship and expects us to be on the same page when we start off using the G-word. But I don't think we are.

At an airport bar in Toronto, not long before 9/11 and between the Bush Wars, I was sitting between a Kuwaiti gentleman and a born-again Christian from Texas. The Kuwaiti, a young college graduate, was gulping down Johnny Walkers at an impressive rate and lamenting that when he got home this drinking would have to end. He also gave an appreciative nod at some females at the bar, implying he was going to miss Western women, too. He ended his soliloquy with an admission that he would, eventually, have to atone for the sinful habits he had acquired here in the West and, now that he had learned the "evil ways of the world," he was ready to return to his native land and take on "the responsibilities of manhood." With a sigh, he conceded that now was as good a time as any.

I let the conversation meander. I got him talking about the separation of church and state here in the West, something that was achieved at tremendous human expense over hundreds of years—the Reformation, the Renaissance, the Enlightenment, the Age of Reason, etc.—and whether or not he thought such a transformation feasible in the Middle East. Feasible, perhaps, but desirable? No. He thought a more tolerant society was ultimately what made all this Western hedonism and decadence possible, that by defining Western culture as undeniably hedonistic and decadent we had reached some mutually agreed-upon condemnation. I wasn't in the mood to challenge him; I found his perspective intriguing, if paradoxical.

Suddenly, I shit you not, the Texan, who had been listening to all this with one eye on the *Monday Night Football* broadcast on the TV over the bar, asked the young Muslim, "But you have accepted Jesus Christ as your personal Savior, have you not?" It was unclear whether the Texan meant all Muslims or our young friend specifically, but that distinction hardly seemed to matter. I will spare you the painful recitation of the ensuing conversation except to say that the young man showed grace, poise, patience, and the eloquence one can only achieve through repetition, as he explained that Mohammed, not Christ, was at the center of his faith. Listening to this and seeing they were at an impasse, I bought us another round and brought in my favorite mediator, quoting him as best I could, saying, "Gandhi suggested that these are all just different paths leading to the same place, right?"

Simultaneously and without hesitation, the Muslim from Kuwait and the born-again Christian from Texas, *and my pal Gordo*, to whom I had been telling this story by way of illustration, all replied, "No, they are not."

I answered Gordo the same way I answered my friends at the bar, "Then the only outcome of that view is war."

Gordo is a good and fast talker and his silences are almost always meant to imply a readiness to listen. We have been friends, enemies, partners, adversaries, and drinking buddies. He wants me to drag him into a loftier exchange than the one I had with those two men at the bar in Toronto. So I ramble on about the human impulse to mythologize what is a natural proclivity for abstract thought, and my view that, as far as mankind has come since the Enlightenment, it wouldn't take much of a collapse in the progress of Reason to plunge humanity into another Dark Age. For me, that was the real danger behind Reagan's abandonment of education and his lending political legitimacy to his evangelical supporters.

Gordo has more faith than I in the resiliency of the idea of progress and the strength of the status quo, but is willing to hear me out. I suggest that, historically, times aren't always as flush as they have been in post-WWII America, the era in which our attitudes were formed; that in ideologically uncertain times, rational cosmological curiosities devolve into irrational, primitive suppositions, and our hopes and fears step in to fill the gaps in our thinking, thereby flirting with a dangerous cultural formula for a return to barbarism. In other words we create, at times, mythologies to get at the heart of the heretofore unexplainable; we create superstitions to compensate for our ignorance.

"So you're saying that God is either a myth or a superstition?" Gordo asks wearily, very nearly doing that TV thing of summing up what someone is saying by throwing some of their own words back at them. I'm not biting.

"Well, I think that, historically, institutions have attempted to anthropomorphize the concept of God into some sort of politically viable entity." I add that superstition has played a role in setting comprehensible, if false, limits in the world. Because current knowledge and the ability to hypothesize will only take the observer so far out in space and time before he or she becomes lost and must seek to grope his or her way back to familiar territory. A territory to which, once having left, ideologically speaking, there is really no return.

"A point of no return, like Eden," he says, sounding truly glum.

"A point of no return can be a good thing, too. Do we want to return to inquisitions and holocausts?"

I can hear Gordo scratching his beard on the other end of the phone. A good sign. Gordo is a videotape editor and so it is his job to take long swaths of images and cut them into quick, snappy little phrases. In fact, I can hear him clicking buttons on his tape console as we speak. I can also hear him taking chunks of ice into his mouth from a plastic cup and crunching them loudly right in my ear. I can practically see his eyes darting back and forth from one monitor to the other, making professional and aesthetic judgments simultaneously as we speak. I'm beginning to get the idea that he's been editing a particularly nasty bit of footage today, parts of which we peons here in the general public will never see. He points out that inquisitions and holocausts are still happening around the world, we're just calling them different things, like "jihad," or "ethnic cleansing." He sounds like he is trapped in one of his endless video loops. Like a squirrel in a cage. We have somehow put God at the center of a wheel and every time we think we are getting close, we find ourselves traveling back out a different spoke, toward an inevitable encounter with the harsh reality that exists beyond the outer rim. Where the rubber meets the road.

I take a second to think back on all the material currently available and recall out loud that one question on the table these days is, if you abandon a sacred canon of behavior, be it a supposedly God-given set of commandments or a political constitution, without replacing it with a better one, more suited to contemporary needs, won't ethics deteriorate until our deeds become more and more intolerable?

"Questions, questions, questions," Gordo heaves one of his more dramatic sighs. "Abstract thought is the basis of imagination." He embarks upon a ramble of his own, returning to something I was getting at earlier. But he sounds a bit peeved. Maybe he doesn't like thinking about God as an abstraction. Maybe he doesn't like what he's seeing on his television screen. He also likes to quote Voltaire in reminding me that "if God didn't exist, mankind would be forced to invent him," and the conundrum posed by his university theosophy teacher that "atheists first must *believe* there is a God *not* to believe in."

Gordo thinks that last piece of sophistry cleverer than I do. Meanwhile, I am trying to keep that mysterious unmentioned video footage in mind. It could be the reason he has suddenly found himself in a moral quandary. Of course, if I were to ask specifically what he's working on that minute, he would brush me off with yet another sigh, exhaling some platitude about the endless tedium and sameness of his grueling, thankless efforts. He will spare me those remarks if I let him. But I remind myself, before pushing on, that sooner or later he's going to have to return his full attention to his work. I worm my way back to the topic at hand by reminding him that the imagination is a valuable problem-solving tool when tempered with reason. It is rarely trustworthy when sparked solely by emotion, and becomes what Western Enlightenment philosophers would call the enemy of reason; what fundamentalists of all stripes have always called the enemy of faith.

"So you're saying that religion and science are both suspect?"

This takes me by surprise. I hadn't given any thought to the age-old debate between science and religion. The TV screen in my mental picture of Gordo's workstation has just flipped from the horrors of Bosnia to the moral debate over funding NASA when there are starving people in the world.

"Um, yeah. Sometimes. Maybe. I mean, a medicine man in a primitive tribe can be just as out of ideas as a contemporary scholar who suggests we are at the end of history, don't you think?"

Silence.

"But look, we've gotten off track here," I say, trying to pull up. "What I grapple with when I consider this stuff is more or less what every sentient being has contemplated, either literally or figuratively, over the course of time. And that is: What are the genuine wonders of the fact of consciousness and at what point are they recognizable as such? Where inside us is the link to the self forged that will then reveal that greater link to what we are trying to identify as God? How do I account for the unexplainable paradox of life and death? Or, why does darkness appear so permanent, and light only temporary?"

Admittedly, I tend to blather like a college philosophy major stoned on Budweiser. So does Gordon. We're the guys who corner you at a party after four or five drinks, pointing at your chest and screaming, "And another thing!" But all I'm trying to do here is get him out of Bible class long enough for him to examine his own beliefs without the muddying distractions of dogma, allegory, and politics. Not good enough. Gordo wants me to boil it down for him and that implies that he thinks I have boiled it down for myself. I can't answer the above questions. Heck, I'm happy just to form the sentences. Do you believe or don't you? Gordo wants to ask—but doesn't. Or, more appropriately, he wants me to reach back over the many years of our friendship and remind him if he had once believed at all. Yes or no. Quick, simple, comprehensible. Gordo still believes! Film at eleven.

Instead, I have slowed him down long enough to suggest that, over the past few centuries, and particularly in the last fifty years, the religious institutions that took the spiritual lead in Western society have been forced to loosen their political grip, and, as a result, plenty of trustworthy thinkers are free to approach these subjects with wide-open minds, blending ancient philosophies with contemporary ethical imperatives, all the while keeping their genuine spiritual inclinations intact. No, most of these current ruminators haven't claimed for their ideas the legitimacy of coming direct from some unseen deity. That, to me, is what is so refreshing about their points of view. Philosophically, spiritually, and ethically, collectively, this could be a golden time in the history of ideas. Or it could be an invitation to chaos.

None of this is very satisfying to Gordo who would like some sort of answer now, so he can get on with his day without the universe imploding in around him. He'd call me a deist if he could remember what it meant. He'd realize that he is one as well. Also, it is such an easy topic to exploit, and I know Gordon has unwittingly bought into a discipline that exploits the discourse of society in crude and cruel little chunks. So I'm being careful not to give him a sound bite. Deep down he knows that. This is why he comes to me when his foundations start to quake. Why, too, that I rarely hear from him when he's doing well. I guess what I'm saying is that I don't sense an open mind but, as with so many of us, a door that is only slightly ajar. Pried open by the inevitable panic we all feel from time to time.

When Gordo and I hang up the phone, we have agreed to get together and talk about God sometime. I smile for a moment, staring out my office window. I thought we just had.

The Conjecture Chamber

manda Gay is dead.

I don't like to muse about death. As a reference point for the varying propositions regarding life it can be useful, but I have never entertained the fascination that seems to obsess so many. I will be forced to deal with its many aspects soon enough.

I'm standing on the Metro platform in The Capital of the Empire, Washington, D.C. I'm waiting for the subway far beneath the business district. I'm trying not to think about Amanda Gay when suddenly I notice that the fellow standing next to me seems very uncomfortable. Curious, because he's got to be wearing five thousand dollars' worth of clothes. A camel hair coat. Italian loafers with tassels. He's carrying an umbrella and briefcase. Beneath the coat is a blue suit, white shirt, red tie. The Kakistocracy Uniform. He appears about twenty-five pounds overweight. His hair is professionally coiffured. He is approximately my age—that is to say, nearing forty. He is perfect. A perfect example of the white-collar class of fatuous, self-absorbed, self-important, ill-informed, unread, culturally inert pigs that you find lurking around centers of money and power.

I am a working musician playing two hundred nights a year. Just one other musician and I tour together, write all our material, and book and promote the gigs as well. I've lost my patience with people who don't support the arts, never go out, read crap, and presume their financial status to be the sum and substance of their societal prerequisites. I've had a thousand and one encounters with arse-holes like him. Pick a topic and he'll spit back some arbitrary gibberish he's heard shouted from his TV, or hit you with his who cares, so what kind of apolitical cynicism that prides itself on looking out for number one yet denudes his personality of any individually inspired content whatsoever. The reactionary expressions he shares with his peers will vary, but the overall smug, peevish sentiments are the same with all these guys. I used to indulge these fellows. I used to give them the benefit of the doubt. I used to have a do unto others as you would have them do unto you attitude. But no more. They've done unto me enough. They've taken over. They are the enemy. Now I openly challenge them every chance I get. Lead Belly was right, I think to myself as I click my teeth with disgust, this is a bourgeois town.

Single women outnumber single men here in the Capital of the Empire. An intriguing statistic. When I hear these women bemoan the fact that all the good ones are taken, I think it's absurd until I catch a glimpse of guys like this. He's a good one. I'm sure he's taken. I look for his ring finger, but he is wearing gloves. I am about to turn away in search of some more pleasant preoccupation when I think of other empire capitals throughout history and wonder what the merchant classes of those eras were like. I wonder how similar or different this son-of-a-bitch is from them. How does he stack up? I try to imagine myself standing on a London railway platform circa 1890, or in Constantinople, or Rome, Paris, Tokyo, Berlin, Athens, Ayodhya, Alexandria, Beijing, all at the height of empire. Now, this specimen seems quite interesting. A real live artifact. On another day, in a better mood, I might have tried to strike up a conversation with him. I could go into my affable kook routine I use on stage to disarm him and draw him out. Maybe see if I could come away with some identifying quotes. Some kind of watermark I could then cut and paste into something useful. A caricature of our times. Then I suddenly know why he's uncomfortable. He's afraid that is exactly what I am about to do.

As soon as I get on the train, my mind is on something else. Seven stops later I exit the subway, pick up my car, and arrive at the Royal Mile Pub early, so I must wait for my friends. The Royal Mile isn't my idea of the perfect bar. The tables are too big and too close together. The lights are always bright, and there is no place to hide. Nor am I impressed by their infinite selection of beer. I would never come here on my own with a good book and my journal. I feel conspicuous, and the short wait is excruciating.

Amanda Gay was a beauty, but I didn't lust after her as did every other male in her immediate orbit. On the contrary, I've always found giant breasts humorous in the extreme. Some women don't like being made love to by a fellow who can't stop giggling. She was a musical stylist, had a unique way of rearranging popular songs in their flat or sharp keys. Whenever we were playing in the same burg, she would seek me out and we would sneak off for a quiet drink and a chat. She would hold my hand. We were at a hotel bar during a convention of college-booking agents once when some kid wearing his ball cap backwards, knee-length shorts, and sneakers that didn't match, approached her drunkenly and without once making eye contact with her said in a loud voice, "Hellacious tits!" I put down my drink and was reaching for his throat when she stood up majestically, pulled back her shoulders, and raised his chin to meet his poor vapid gaze, and without a trace of gratitude said, "Thank you."

My friends arrive and the frenzy begins. These are tough-nosed, school of hard knocks, self-employed people who see the world differently than most corporate or government employees. Most people have to do the job hunt boogie half a dozen times in their lives. Self-employed individuals essentially have to look for work every day. Jaded, edgy, and angry, they have a very practical appreciation of how things do and do not work; of whom they can and cannot trust. They also have a deep and abiding loyalty to anyone who ever got them a gig, made them a sale, or sent a hot prospect their way. We have all met through our various professions. We enjoy each other's company, but we will never be what you might call close. That's fine with us. Somewhere deep down, we all know that before long we will disperse, that life's imperatives will carry us away from one another. We've also reached an age where death is more and more likely. So we know how to savor the moment.

Cid is a real estate agent. Divorced. Unlike most real estate scum, he's a real bright guy, but he just walks around enraged all the time. He blows up at stupid and inept retail clerks. Warm beer makes him furious. During the first Gulf War, those "We Support Our Troops" banners would make him go berserk. "How many people are you willing to kill to remain dependent on foreign oil? You! I mean you, personally, how many?" he would accost some unsuspecting patriot. Everywhere Cid looks he sees inanity and stupidity closing in around him. His healthy reflex is to lash out to create neutral space for himself. As soon as he sits down, he's at it again, red-faced over some idiot in the parking lot. I order a half-and-half and make an attempt to alter the course of his harangue. What's the use of challenging every damn fool in your path? I argue, forgetting the fight I was dying to pick with the dweeb on the Metro platform. Cid has been practicing Zen for a while. He says it's to calm him down, but I feel it has contributed to his frustrations. I'm not sure it's wise to integrate universes, metaphysically, I mean. Being Aware is one thing, but trying to bring that Other, which is surmise at best, to some intersection with the corporeal is potentially dangerous, if you ask me. It certainly hasn't calmed Cid down any.

Earl Riles is another one. Another musician. A perfectionist. He gets in these incredible funks. Hates everybody. He wears black all the time, and, although several people at the bar have recognized him, he is oblivious. Tonight we'll all troop back to his place and sit up drinking Pernod and he'll just let it all out. The world, according to Earl, is a place without love. He believes romance is pathetic. This belief renders him hopelessly romantic to his dark legion of followers. He, too, sees uselessness and dreck everywhere he looks. All Earl wants is a little recognition and respect. When he gets it, he finds it to be hideous and deformed. He wants to lash out as well. But at what? I've been hearing these laments all my life and I wonder about the syndrome at large.

As this familiar rant reaches its apogee, I'm trying to remember a passage from Henry Miller's *The Air-Conditioned Nightmare*, penned in 1944:

As to whether I have been deceived, disillusioned... The answer is yes, I suppose. I had the misfortune to be nourished by the dreams and visions of great Americans—the poets and seers. Some other breed of man has won out. This world which is in the making fills me with dread. I have seen it germinate; I can read it like a blue-print. It is not a world I want to live in. It is a world suited for monomaniacs obsessed with the idea of progress—but a false progress, a progress which stinks. It is a world cluttered with useless objects which men and women, in order to be exploited and degraded, are taught to regard as useful. The dreamer whose dreams are not utilitarian has no place in this world. Whatever does not lend itself to being bought and sold, whether in the realm of things, ideas, principles, dreams or hopes, is debarred. In this world the poet is anathema, the thinker a fool, the artist an escapist, the man of vision a criminal.

I perceive the same sense of abandonment in Cid and Earl. I feel it too, somewhat. Cid, Earl, and I are lucky in that we are able to stay mobile. I am always on the road. Cid likes to travel and Earl gets gigs twice a year in Europe, where they treat him like an artist rather than an ornament or an afterthought as they do here in the States.

Agnes has joined us and is taking us all in with a grain of salt and a shot of tequila. She waits to get a word in edgewise and then informs us that she has problems too. Her boyfriend has dumped her. "Good riddance!" we all agree, then vote to move on to another topic. Not good enough. Agnes wants a pound of male flesh, but she's come to the wrong place. We're only willing to cough up an ounce apiece. Why are men like this? Where is he? Have we seen him? He must have another girl. That's it, isn't it? You guys are protecting him! What an asshole thing to do!

"The problem we have here," I interrupt, "is that you're the dump-ee and he is the dump-er."

"I've been dumped on all right!"

"Well, yes, but you see, in this situation, when you are the dump-ee, all you are left holding onto are a lot of worthless conjectures. Where is he? Where did you go wrong?, etc. It's like this big iron door slams shut on you, and you're locked in this deep dark Conjecture Chamber where the most complicated personal questions are posed and, since you are suddenly cut off from the data flow, out of the loop, those questions can only be answered hypothetically by your deepest fears and insecurities. These horrific negative scenarios are displayed over and over as if on a big-screen TV for your own private torment. No good can come from spending time in the Conjecture Chamber. What's worse is, the longer you stay in there, the further from reality you stray. So, when and if you do emerge, the further you have to go to make it back."

"Okay, that's exactly where I am. Now how do I get out?"

"You have to change the subject, but it doesn't occur to you to change the subject when you're in the Conjecture Chamber because that's not the Conjecture Chamber's function. So something has to be randomly introduced that changes the subject naturally."

"Like getting rid of the hiccups," Cid says to Earl, tossing him a wink.

"It's pitiful being the dump-ee. I wish he would take me back just so I could dump him and see how he likes it in there," she scowls. Now she's slid from anger to depression. She turns to Cid for some positive reenforcement, but his divorce has left him cynical and broke all the time. When he realizes it's his turn to speak, he shrugs and says, "Look, you're in love. You thought he would be different."

A heavy silence descends.

Agnes watches that weight settle on our brows, then lets us know she isn't finished. Cid's last remark has pissed her off again. She is dangerously close to tossing the lot of us in the same boat with her despised lost love. "Men—you're all brain damaged at birth. It's a scientific fact. Did you know that?"

She's got our attention.

"I've always suspected it was something like that," I say, trying to humor her but a little afraid that she might be onto us.

"It's true. In the womb we all begin as females, then, when the first jolt of testosterone gushes through the forming corpus callosum it turns you into males and turns your brains to shit. All of you. Shit for brains. That's what I'm going to call him from now on. Shit for Brains." That said, she looks at us defiantly, awaiting rebuttal. We look at each other stupidly and launch into a discussion of contemporary films.

Cid quit going to the movies years ago. Can't remember the last film he went to see. "They're all made for adolescents. Superheroes, pirates, cartoons, and TV sitcoms pretending to be movies. Films made for people my age are about depraved serial killers or drug addicts. I have zero interest in or empathy for either."

Amanda Gay's death has jerked my mind around in another direction. I'm thinking of a worrisome spate of films that have come out in the past decade also aimed at teenagers. Films like *Mr. Destiny*, *Ghost*, *Ghost Dad*, *Weekend at Bernie's*, *Weekend at Bernie's II*, and a whole bunch more, all with this cavalier, sophomoric, thoughtless attitude toward death. It's healthy, I think, to whistle past the graveyard, but these films take us somewhere else. Death as adolescent situation comedy. Death as cartoon. Death as just another bogus adventure in our frivolous and bogus lives. No discovered nugget of wisdom; no mirrored image of obvious truth revealed. It's a classic bait and switch: a quest for frivolous sex is interrupted by an equally frivolous death. As superficial and interchangable as shopping and fucking. Love and death. Shopping and fucking. And where do young people go to see these films? Shopping malls.

Agnes comes bursting out of the Conjecture Chamber with a vengeance. Her expertise is in urban planning, and if there's one thing that can set her blood to boiling it's shopping malls. She sees them as the perfect link between corporate television advertising and consumers, without the disturbing notion of community and social responsibility interfering with the exchange of funds from lower class to higher. You needn't feel responsible for buying your shoes from the local retailer who is also your neighbor because there is no longer a local shoe retailer. And your neighbor? Screw him. You've never even met.

Cid unexpectedly takes a turn in the Conjecture Chamber wondering why it is so. Why do people frown on the solid urban brick dwellings built to last a century, downtown, where everything is convenient and you don't even need a car, to the prefab claptrap pasteboard houses that cost twice as much?

Earl is eating it up. He launches a rant of his own. The opposite of love is not hate, but death. And into this loveless universe, the one Agnes's ex-boyfriend has jettisoned her, and now all of us, into, the anxious citizens of the world will live in a music-less hateful ugly void that they so richly deserve.

I abandon them to their joyous nihilism to watch a hockey game on the bar's television, keeping one ear on the conversation lest it turn carnivorous.

"Yes, you *can* take it with you!" is the subliminal corporate message being insidiously injected into our doped-up psyches. Alone and unloved, our culture has been driven to the edge of an abyss we are only dimly aware of. Why? Because the consciousness of the hive is stupefied and two dimensional.

Don't tell Mom, the babysitter is dead.

Miller was right, we were nourished by great American poets and seers. He was one himself. But as I look around the room all I see are Earl, Agnes, Cid, and myself among the yuppie drones. Earlier post–World War II eras had their intellectual heroes. Ginsberg, and Kerouac, Adlai Stevenson, Bob Dylan, Dick Gregory, Gene McCarthy, Hunter Thompson, Rock'n'Roll. Now we look around and realize we have only each other. The field is barren. We have, for tonight at any rate, formed an inebreational Star Chamber in which Amanda would have felt right at home. We have broken on the wheel of our mutual anxieties the poor, guilty, overpaid slob from the Metro platform, who is just one of the many co-conspirators threatening to bring darkness down upon our life and times. For the remainder of the night the Conjecture Chamber door will remain open, and we enter and exit at will. Politics, mysticism, and human relations are played out upon its grand screen. We agree to recognize the possibility that a new dark age may well be upon us but at least we'll not have to face it alone.

We break it up at five a.m. I stumble out of Earl's place as delightfully pickled as a fellow can be. I remove the T-top from my Oldsmobile, fire up a cigar, pop a fresh brewski, and cruise home through the park. The tall lush trees of the Empire Capital undulate luxuriously in the cool springtime air. Amanda loved the T-top. She would designate me her chari-oteer, undo our seat belts, and curl up next to me on the bench seat, knees drawn up, her crazy hair whipping my face as we blazed through the summer night. Now, the angst, hubris, and delirium of the evening have already fallen from me like old skin. Amanda was killed four months ago, a few days after the New Year. She was jogging, wearing headphones. Got struck by a car. She carried no ID on her run, so she lay in a morgue for months as a Jane Doe until at last her parents found her. Two thousand admirers and fans went to her funeral. I only heard of it the other day when asking an agent from her home-town Chicago what she was up to. I had sent her a card saying, "Have A Hellacious Holiday."

I blow her a kiss from my dark and happy night.

My Haunted Crucifix

It was positioned next to a secondary altar, forward and off to the right from the main one, nearer to the communion rail and therefore nearer to the congregation, in the old gothic church of my youth: a crucifix of such startling realism it would stop anyone cold whose eyes fell upon it for the first time. I knew people who avoided that side of the church altogether, or would avert their eyes while passing by, gazing down at the blood-red carpet, or into the distance opposite, over the rows of handcrafted wooden pews. Each time I saw it, I was so horrified as to be transfixed. It called to me, drew me to it as a fallen stranger draws a Good Samaritan. Thinking of it now gives me chills and makes me reach for a comforting image, yet none is so palliative as to provide solace from all the dread this memory conveys.

The Shrine of the Most Blessed Sacrament, where I attended grade school, is a small enclave of Catholic worship and education adjacent to Chevy Chase Circle in Washington, D.C. The school, church, and convent where the Sisters of the Sacred Heart reside form a universe unto themselves for the parishioners and children whose lives are centered around it. Like most Catholic kids growing up in the 1950s and early '60s, I have my stories to tell. But when I think of that time in my life, when I think of that school and my experiences there growing up, I return again and again to this crucifix. I believe it has a great deal to do with the forming of my political and psycho-sexual persona as I moved from frightened child to curious young adult to grown man.

The figure of Christ was unusual because it was so large. Most crucifixes are small enough to be placed on a wall or altar, or carried in a procession. Miniatures will fit onto the end of a pocket rosary. But this one was almost as big as I was. In other words, it was the size of a child. I identified first with this size, I think. Christ's head was bowed, his eyes half-open as though he had just uttered his last, "It is finished." His was a sublime and intelligent countenance. The sadness in that face haunts me still, for it contained disappointment, an ultimate despair; in a certain sense, the face even exuded failure. The body was pale, thin, with ribs that stuck out. If this man lived on the alms of others, he was disappointed in life as well as death. The grime and uncleanliness resulting from his mistreatment, the whip marks reaching around his torso from the scourging the night before, the loincloth that barely clung to his protruding hips, these spoke volumes about the human capacity for suffering at the hands of others. His poor, blood-clotted fingers clung pitifully to the nails that jutted out from his palms. He was hanging on, the tendons in his arms straining to lighten the burden of his body's weight. The thorns of his crown were very long and ghastly sharp, and each one sent long tears of blood down that sad face.

A crucified person dies of asphyxiation. When you are no longer able to hold your head up, you bow your head and suffocate. He had had a rough couple of days. He was tired. It didn't take as long as it might have to die.

On Fridays I would emerge from the confessional and, while other children went back to their pews to giggle and pretend to say their prayers, I would advance to the side altar where this crucifix was mounted on the gray concrete wall and kneel there, looking up at him. I would study the beautiful figure of the man himself. His feet, delicate, lay impossibly one atop the other to meet the wooden board to which they were nailed with one spike. The indignity of his exposed and public encounter with death was embarrassing and humiliating in the pre–sexual revolution 1950s, even for a witness. Caught in his sighing last breath, he found even there an opportunity to utter a final complaint about the way we live our lives.

Spread out before him in that stodgy, cavernous, and darkly ornate old church was the self-assured, fully clothed congregation: those spiteful, glowering, bitter, haughty, and arrogant nuns; and the priests, always striking a benign and beneficent pose but ever vigilant, like quiet lieutenants of an unseen or unknown commander. Before them all, dressed in their sanctimonious garbs, the uniforms and raiments of society, the figure on the cross was so *naked*.

After I grew up, I was for many years a traveling professional musician. A fellow musician, a Jew, surprised to see me reading the Old Testament before turning in one night after a gig on the road, asked me a question he had always wanted to ask a gentile. Did I blame the Jews for killing Jesus? No, I answered, it had never occurred to me to think there was blame to assert, or that it even mattered. The emphasis in our Catholic teaching had been on the greater reasons for his life and death—becoming flesh and blood, walking among us, forgiving our sins. He needed to die in this way to accomplish his mission. Had he died in an accident, or contracted a disease, the whole story would have been different.

Besides, I always had the impression that Jesus was killed by neither the Romans nor the Jews. I always believed it was God, the Father, who was responsible for the death of Jesus. "Why hast thou forsaken me?" is a question countless children have asked of their fathers over the millennia, or of their guardians whenever they've found themselves at the mercy of a hierarchy of self-serving pharisees or the tyrannical jurisprudence of a greedy misanthropic bureaucracy.

My many hours of contemplation looking up at that crucifix, the penances I performed at its bloody broken feet, shaped in part my future politics: my distrust of the state and of religious institutions, my revulsion at capital punishment and the power of life and death over its citizens that the state claims as justified and God given. But more than that, sometimes I would gaze at the opulence of those surroundings, and hear the words of faith, hope, and charity parroted by the congregation, and contrast this with the fate of this poor pitiful man, naked and nailed to boards, dying in front of all these supposedly pious souls. I would wonder, was I the only one in the room to see the contradiction here? Yet, one classical message did get through to me. His flesh instructed my soul in ways in which to "offer it up."

The concept of "offering it up," I was startled to learn when I moved beyond the boundaries of my Catholic upbringing, was not a universal teaching. At least I've not encountered it elsewhere. We were constantly told by our educators and parents that the sufferings we endure in this life were put there to inform and instruct us, but more importantly to test our faith. These sufferings could be offered up to God as a kind of sacrifice—other than our sacrifices, what have we, really, as representative offerings of our virtues? I have always thought the missing concept of sacrifice is what gives the lie to the devotion of televangelists and born-agains: their brand of Christianity is simply too easy without it. If the cross is where life leads us, this Christian way of life should not be easy.

I did not think of the religious icons in the church as objects of art when I was a child. Kids would ask, if idolatry was wrong, why do we kneel and pray before a statue? Of course, the explanation was that these were not idols, but icons to keep our attention focused. People knelt and prayed before the symbols of their faith. Thus an early moral quandary was averted. But doesn't one quandary always lead to others?

When I consider Christ's dilemma for any length of time, I simply find the Church's explanation for the necessity of his martyrdom inadequate. Why was this gentle soul held down and nailed to these boards in the first place? When I ponder the implications of a dogma-driven culture, the facts of the story as told by the four apostles in the New Testament, and the sociopolitical forces that assumed it was all right, and even necessary, to torture and murder him, I can only conclude that, given the right circumstances, we are all eligible for such treatment.

When I consider the politics of a Roman occupation, and of a Pontius Pilate, I think of the entrenched Jewish leadership of the region and their fear of succession. I think of the kind of societal machinations practiced by those with power, as well as those attempting to achieve power. I then shudder at how easy it is to fall afoul of all those interests, as have political prisoners all over the world, from jailed marijuana users in the United States to enemies of juntas in South America, Africa, China, and elsewhere.

In the mid-1980s, my Jewish musical partner and I attended a Bob Dylan concert at a big stadium. It was during Dylan's Christian phase, and he was sharing the stage with Tom Petty and the Heartbreakers. It was a terrific show, and the last, I think, of what I would call Dylan's "howling years." When Dylan strode to the microphone and sang the words, "When they came for him in the garden, did they know?" a sweet song about the moment of Christ's betrayal, my friend sought me out in the crowd and, with eyes bulging from his head in anger, screamed, "What the hell is this?"

"Calm down," I patted his back as we watched. "Think of Jesus as a metaphor for every poor innocent fuck who's been dragged from his home and shot in the streets for his beliefs." At the time, Ronald Reagan was not so secretly funding the Contras in Central America. One of their tactics was to go into a village and drag all the men from their homes and murder them in front of their families. From then on, my pal had no problem listening to Dylan's Christian material.

As for me, I am forever kneeling on that velvet cushion at the magnificent mahogany railing in that dark old church beneath my haunted crucifix, where candles for the dead are always burning, where everything has its own elegiac echo—even the whispering zephyr-like swish from the long black robes of the nuns as they move so swiftly and lightly on their feet, and the sound of the long rosaries hooked onto their ropey belts clacking gently at their sides. Sometimes the sisters hold their rosaries in one hand to silence them. They move about, gliding, watching, always enforcing a hush on us potentially rowdy children.

This is not a warm and welcoming place. It is cavernous and gray with red velvet and gold. It is heavy dark wood and cement and stone. Scrutiny was constant. Every movement was watched and considered, and make no mistake, the scrutiny was there not to protect us, but to protect the estate in which we found ourselves.

Once, in grade school, I was assaulted by a bully who tried to throw me over a railing at the top of a long flight of marble stairs. A friend who intervened convinced me to report the incident. The bully's parents were major contributors to the parish. I was the one who was ultimately punished. Over the years, whenever their word went up against mine, I stood my ground, and I lost. My fellow students would abandon me to my fate, apologizing in private for not wanting to get in trouble. But that's what it was all about—fear. Scaring you into being good. They knelt you down in front of that horrific crucifix. They hovered over you and watched what you did and listened to what you said. "Good" had a metaphysical definition in the catechism, but was in practice a mere euphemism for conformity. Back in class we talked a lot about hell, where they would hurt you forever if you were bad. But bad was defined as disobeying rules that could and would be changed arbitrarily.

I eventually came to see the church building itself as merely an expensive imitation of a theater, a hollow space into which were drawn all the vanities, fears, pretensions of status, and covetousness of its congregants, who were, simply, a reflection of its own all-too-human makeup. A space where the human condition was acknowledged only in the most discriminating and incriminating of terms, and where one's membership in the congregation was a discorporate event. Above all, it was clear that when the institution was challenged, it would always look out for its own interests first, that of its benefactors second, and the interests of the rest of us? Not at all.

As an altar boy during Mass, I would kneel at the priest's feet, put my nose to the floor, and spit out the Latin phrases, competing with the other boys for speed and clarity. The priest would listen during his own perfunctory recitations and grade us afterwards. During the homily I would look around the room as the sermon dragged on and wonder, "Are these people really buying this?" Not the words of Christ, of course, but the interpretation of those who came after. Paul, the tax collector turned convert, was the one everyone in authority seemed to relate to most. I reasonably concluded it was really Paul we were all to emulate, not Jesus. If we were all to really emulate Christ, we would have to get up and leave this place with its gold candleholders and rubied chalices, throw off these raiments of status, and be other than what we were. Paul was a very acceptable substitute. We could all choose to be Paul, though not just yet. I would sit with my parents in the congregation and listen to the mighty organ play in the choir loft above, entertaining us while the collection baskets were solemnly passed. The laymen were severe, efficient, and precise in the execution of their duty. The parents all had their collection envelopes, personalized and numerically coded, so there would be no mistaking on the holy ledger who had given what. At the beginning of each school year, the kids received their own color-coded envelopes, marked by gender, marked for Sundays and Feast Days. Always the sly, greedy, and malevolent eye was upon us.

When I was in kindergarten, I had a crush on a little girl in my class. Go ahead and laugh, if you will, but when the parish stepped in to forbid my family from throwing a mixed gender birthday party for me, I was astonished. I went to church and watched the priest, I went to school and watched the teacher, but it hadn't occurred to me that school and church were watching back, that they were taking an active role in my life, or that they could mess with me. I never trusted them again, and I've been suspicious of socially meddlesome politics ever since.

In the long run, however, it didn't matter who was watching. When there is no authority figure handy to observe your actions, or when you find yourself beyond the normal reach of the mechanized accounting system that deems whether you are indeed behaving properly, there is always the greatest eye of all: God Himself. And once you have accepted the fiction of an omnipotent being invading your cranium, commandeering your imagination, and governing your behavior by robbing you of your privacy, isn't it then a short leap in logic to accepting a flesh-and-blood Big Brother in the real world? Ultimately, what's most important to know is that you cannot act unobserved.

As I grew up, getting to know the self-perpetuating nature of human institutions, the petty irrational paranoias they harbor and manifest, and the resulting violence they are capable of inflicting on innocent people, I was not surprised that they, whoever "they" were, had taken this most beautiful of God's human creations, this fellow called Jesus, and done this to him. For me, the crucifix also represents the God-condoned, church-condoned, state-sanctioned sacrilege against human beauty, nature, and sensuality. For the desecration of tenderness, and the putting to filth that which is inherently clean, tells me all I need to know about God, the State, and the company they both keep.

Ultimately, what happened to Jesus is actually celebrated. And if it be condoned and celebrated for the Son of God, then it will be condoned and celebrated for all sons and daughters of all deities everywhere. You and I. Is there a word in English, or any language, for the urge to destroy things that are beautiful? Perhaps we should create a new term for this kind of shame: *Beauticide.*

As I grew physically and intellectually within the institutions of Church and State, I treated virtually everything these authoritarians told me, from the sum of two plus two to their definition of God, with the greatest skepticism. Like a theater-goer who sees the same play night after night, eventually I lost my ability to suspend disbelief, and I began to see the workings of this most deceptive art. I watched as political leaders in the secular world boisterously claimed that by virtue of their newfound religious devotions they too could assume a degree of infallibility. What a scam. The sum of two plus two I can figure out, but whenever I become smug or cozy in my own sanctimonious revelations regarding all things political or metaphysical, all I have to do is kneel down at that altar rail and gaze up.

To please my mother in the years before she died, I would attend Catholic Mass with her once a year on Easter Sundays.

It had been decades since I had last been there. When we sat down in our old church, the first thing I looked for was that crucifix. It was gone. After Mass I sought out a church volunteer, a man I remembered from those early days, now grown old, and asked where it had gone. He said that people had complained about it, and so it was taken down and stored in the basement.

I know that basement. It is where, as altar boys, we used to change clothes. It is a cramped, dry, sepulcher. Now, I think of the contemporary Catholic service, the priest facing the congregation instead of turning his back. English instead of Latin. The parishioners hold the Body of Christ in their hands, when to touch the host when we were kids could get you expelled from school. Being a Catholic is easier than it once was. I think of that crucifix in the basement. Little altar boys—and girls—are getting undressed and dressed in front of it. I would advise them to take a good long look.

I wish them well.

The International Aeronautical Sanitation Administration

(or what to do with our nuclear and toxic waste before it kills us all)

Free advice for the Mescalero Indians of New Mexico: Get some dogs, a shovel, and a really big freezer. Also, if your town starts to smell like dirty socks—move.

I have begun this essay in response to the news that some Native Americans in the Southwestern United States are hoping to make big bucks by turning over their hard-won land to the federal government for the purpose of storing nuclear waste. Regardless of how the controversy is resolved, or how much money does or doesn't change hands, there will remain a sense of desperation on all sides of this issue.

Listen.

Several years ago, while a member of the political satire musical duet, The Pheromones, I found myself playing a gig at Richland Community College in Richland, Washington. Until our trip to Richland, any thoughts I had about the state of Washington were of fog-draped cities, snow-covered volcanoes, and very big, very old trees. We saw some big mountains and trees but mostly what we found were smaller mountains covered with tree stumps, the barren high desert, and the stink of dirty socks. Richland, you see, is located in the southeast corner of the state, far from any mountains or trees, miles above sea level, and adjacent to the U.S. Department of Energy's Hanford Reservation—for now, probably the biggest known nuclear waste dump in the world.

We were prepared not to like Richland. We brought our own water. The first thing we noticed as we rolled into town in the middle of the night was that the place smelled as if the whole town were involved in some sort of cultlike nocturnal aerobic ceremony which must have concluded minutes before our arrival. When I asked people the next day about the odor in the atmosphere, they looked puzzled. (Much the same way New Yorkers do when you mention the quality of their atmosphere. New Yorkers will tell you there is no smog in New York City, although they will concede that it has been overcast lately. "Haze," I think is the word they use. They presume that it emanates from the steamy, primitive, provincial inland regions. All you can do is humor them.)

Richland, as you have already surmised, is a misnomer; a very bad bit of subliminal municipal name-giving perpetrated, I'm sure, to put people, and I mean innocent, decent, churchgoing, tax-paying, Winnebago-riding, map-reading, voting Americans, off its foul boot stench. I mean, you look at the map, and there, like some national park, is a big square green patch that reads, "U.S. Department of Energy Hanford Reservation," right next to a little town called Rich Land.

Now, if you live in an Alternative Universe—you know, the one where Jack and Bobby Kennedy spent sixteen years in the White House? Where Martin Luther King became secretary of state in the second JFK administration? Where there was no Vietnam War and therefore no Military Industrial Complex sucking up a trillion dollars of GDP every couple of years; where the Cold War ended by treaty after Kennedy's reelection in 1964; where there was no Johnson, Nixon, Ford, Carter, Reagan, Bush, Clinton, Bush II? You know the one: the Alternative Universe where E. F. Schumacher's *Small Is Beautiful* idea became the wisdom of our policy wonks instead of a target of Corporate Economy drones to defame progressive politicians like Jerry Brown and Fred Harris; where we spent the 1970s and '80s designing and implementing an alternative energy strategy that by the mid-1990s had America and the West energy self-sufficient? Where enough food was grown in the unpolluted oceans to feed the entire planet; where solar panels in space ring the Earth?—well, if that's where you live (and make no mistake about it, if it wasn't for Big Oil and the Arms Industry, that's exactly where we'd be) you might look at the square patch on your North American Road Atlas where the U.S. Department of Energy Hanford Reservation is and say, "Oh! That's where all those way-cool windmills and solar collectors are designed and assembled! Let's take the tour!"

Our performance was scheduled for noon the next day in the student lounge instead of the big concert hall. Just as we were about to go on, a student advisor came up to us and asked if any of our material was focused on environmental issues. "Only when we're not slamming Reagan," I answered. By way of demonstration we broke into our twisted Simon & Garfunkel harmony and sang, "I know your love is toxic but I can't help reaching out to touch you bay-hey-bee!" ("Ecological Disaster," by The Pheromones, from the album *So Far…So What!*) It was pretty tame stuff, now that I look back on it. But one must consider the times before you judge us too harshly. In the 1980s and 1990s, everyone was terrified to squeak out against the Right-Wing Republicans—sort of like now, actually. Still, we didn't have a song with lyrics like, "Quit your jobs, band together, and let's shut the fuckers down before they kill us, bay-hey-bee!" and perhaps for that we should be ashamed. Mind you, however, that American liberal politics is remarkable for the fact that if you dare to take a stand, the people who should most support the gesture will crucify you for not going far enough and then abandon the cause, leaving you helpless and out in the open for the opposition to come and have its way with you. Nevertheless, we were prepared to tell the good children of Richland that back in the Capital of the Empire, thousands of miles distant from this troubled out-post, far removed from the barren high desert of America's post-WWII flirtation with Armageddon, there were two guys ready and more than willing to speak out on their behalf!

Boy, were they gonna love us.

At that point, the student advisor asked us very politely to refrain from any mention of environmental issues as a gesture of kindness to the students, most of whom had a relative or friend who was seriously ill, or dead, from the disease-causing elements radiating from the Hanford Reservation. That was why they were hiring entertainers to come all the way to Richland in the first place. In fact, the reason the show was held during the lunch hour was that so many students had sick relatives and related family obligations after school, it was feared that no one would attend an evening performance in the now-dark concert hall. One comedian—who had played the college just the week before, we were told—had to stop his show because when he started to crack jokes about nuclear power many of the people in the audience began weeping uncontrollably.

So we stood there onstage, singing every stupid cover song we could think of while staring blankly at the clock on the wall at the back of the hall. The kids sat there, the girls with their big hair, and the boys with their ball caps on backwards, and stared blankly back at us.

In the cafeteria after the show, we nervously picked at our free food while we waited to be paid. A cafeteria worker, who also worked part time at the Hanford Reserve, gave us the low-down. He told us that at the Reserve they monitor how badly radiation is escaping the reservation by the use of dogs roaming the grounds. Like canaries in a mine shaft, the dogs, and their droppings, are examined, and eventually, after they get sick and die, the dogs and all their poop are frozen and put in a vault underground. In fact, this guy's job, among other things, was to go around and collect those droppings, and the dead dogs themselves.

Are you hearing and seeing this?

In a vault, underground, are thirty-odd years of dead dogs and all their shit. That, plus mountains of deadly nuclear waste all kept in primitive canisters that leak.

Does this sound like High Science to you?

Homo sapiens has been around, as far as we know, for approximately four million years. About four thousand years ago, they invented the plow. Quick, name the top five events in human history occurring between four million and four thousand years ago. Oh, that's right, you can't. That means that there are 3,996,000 years of human history unaccounted for. I think about this when I hear the usual team of know-nothing journalists and experts-for-hire discussing hazardous waste and what to do with it.

I'm thinking, hey, if the average civilization on this planet is measured in hundreds, not thousands, of years, and, if the history of all known civilizations is somewhere in the neighborhood of four thousand years, and if the end of each civilization typically culminates in the near-total destruction of not only society but also the knowledge, religion, mores, and culture that engendered it, then how reasonable, or even logical, is it to talk about hazardous waste that has a half-life of lethal contamination lasting twenty thousand years? How can any such argument that takes as its premise the acceptance of such a risk as worthy be anything but ludicrous, stupid, criminal, and wrong? After all, we are being forced to accept a hazard that outlasts all of recorded history by a factor of fifty. Think of the minds behind such a thing.

Progressives, feminists, eco-feminists, new world spiritualists, enlightened historians, scientists, concerned citizens, and others seeking insight and solutions to these and other difficulties, both physical and cosmological, are just starting to look into this 3,996,000 years of missing human history. These theorists—revisionists you might call them—suggest that before the invention of the plow, men and women roamed the earth for hundreds of thousands of years as partners, hunting and gathering and sharing the burdens of human existence. The question seems to be just how the hell did anyone let the men take over? There is a lot of finger-pointing going on; a lot of blame-laying. They suggest, further, that the last few thousand years of male dominance is just an anomaly, soon to be corrected by the Darwinian swings of historical necessity; that being a cooperative community of humans is normal and that being barbarous murderers, rapists, and despoilers of the Earth is the exception.

Scholarship aside, I, for one, am willing to say, "Sure, why not? Let Alternative Universes abound!" But I would remind you that before we get to the New Age there's the little matter of the mess we've made of the old one. Those canisters out in Hanford are leaking. Those dogs are shitting, dying, and being frozen. Now listen, I'm not a pet person, but I do care about life, about civilization and its future.

These questions run deep into the origins and to the ends of things, true, but in the end it comes down to need, and the ability to meet the need.

We need to get this shit out of here.

So, where in the world do we put it? It's just hard for me to think that the Mescalero's land is the answer. The truth is, my friends, that there is no safe place on Earth for any of it. Nowhere, no matter what the technology, no matter how long we study the problem.

I must say that after watching Reagan, Bush, Clinton, and Bush II throw away hundreds of billions of dollars on SDI or "Star Wars," a project as ill conceived as the Maginot Line, what I'm about to say shouldn't sound all that farfetched. But first, you must be brave. You must be daring. You must expand your awareness beyond the temporal envelope of contemporary ethics, politics, and accepted degrees of plausibility. You must sit down.

Are you ready?

We must launch these dangerous radioactive materials at the Sun. That's right. And while we're at it, all the chemical weapons, nuclear bombs, toxic waste, and every other asinine, Earth-destroying product of man's puny, power-mongering imagination along with it.

I know, I know, Challenger.

But so what? Even if it takes a hundred years to solve the logistical and technical problems presented by gathering up these materials and reducing them to some shape or form transportable to that great atomic recycler in the sky, take the time. These materials surely aren't going anywhere. Meanwhile, the necessary education, the shift in priorities for the global community of nations, the resulting technological breakthroughs at such a crucial juncture in history should boost civilization to heights I would like to see reached for in my lifetime.

Remember that Alternative Universe? You know, where The Beatles stayed together and The Stones broke up? Where Jimi Hendrix grew into an old blues man reinventing a genre of music, and Jim Morrison became a crooner of time-honored romantic ballads? Where John Wellstone became the Majority Leader of the Senate? Where boredom and cynicism are not mainstream expressions of cultural futility because we can vote for progressives and reformers when the culture needs a change and be sure those votes will count? And further, that those progressives will live to fulfill their mission?

I would like to propose this addition to James J. Patterson's Alternative Universe: we eliminate NASA and reinvent it as "The International Aeronautical Sanitation Administration." *TIASA!* Sounds kind of multicultural, doesn't it?

I recently went online with this idea. I hit a few message boards by way of conducting an informal poll. Here is a sample of the results:

- "That's the sickest idea I've ever heard! Now that we've polluted the Earth, let's go out and pollute outer space!"
- "Why not just send the stuff to China? They're far away and they do atmospheric testing anyway."
- "We may easily fill our largest rockets with contaminants and point them at the sun for a fiery end to them and our waste disposal problems."
- "Super idea! Once we do that perhaps the galactic community will think we're at last getting our shit together and begin to take us seriously."
- "Aim shit at the sun? What if the sun just goes out?"

I won't deny that there's an image problem here, perhaps even a knowledge gap. But I challenge you to come up with a better idea. In the meantime I would advise the Mescalaros to give up on this pitiful scheme. (I'm sure, by the way, there are at least a dozen nature deities who are super-pissed already.) Instead, if they really need the money, they should charge the federal government a naming rights fee to use the name Apache on their killer helicopters. Or the Mescaleros can accept the free advice given above and think seriously of lending their name to the next generation of affordable Geiger counters.

It Isn't Whether You Win or Lose, It's How You Watch the Game

Gabbing with O'Reilly

When O'Reilly was at last awarded his seat at RFK Stadium, I had already been sitting in the one next to it for eleven years. He arrived at his first game carrying a seat cushion and blanket, though it was a warm September afternoon. He was in his fifties, if my memory serves, but ruddy-faced and as excited as a little kid. How long he had been on the waiting list I've now forgotten, but seats rarely came open, and the pace was glacial. The time he put in was measured in decades.

When he saw me, a hippie wearing buckskin, he was crestfallen. It was 1972. George Allen was coach of the Washington Redskins and had them winning for the first time in twenty-five years. Vietnam, Nixon, and the private war between generations and lifestyles in America were raging.

The first couple of years he sat next to me, O'Reilly and I never spoke. He ignored me completely, and that's hard to do in close quarters when everyone is excited and there's so much going on. Harder still with someone like me who gabs constantly about players, stats, and game situations with everyone else around me. If I asked him a direct question about a player on the visiting team, he wouldn't answer.

It was called D.C. Stadium when it first opened. I was eight years old and already a huge fan. My dad took me to the games. His company bought a box of season tickets and he purchased two. Since my birthday is in the third week of September, he would give me the tickets as a birthday present, and he did so for forty-two years. He wasn't a big fan and, as soon as I was old enough to go by myself, he let me have both seats, and encouraged me to go alone, scalp the extra ticket, and use the funds for hotdogs and bus fare.

A couple of years earlier, I had sat crossed-legged on the floor in the basement in front of our black-and-white TV watching Johnny Unitas of the Baltimore Colts beat the New York Giants in overtime during the championship game. I had run upstairs, where the adults were having cocktails, several times, saying, "You need to come down and see this, I think what's happening is really special," to which they smiled and sent me on my way, maybe coming down one at a time, drinks tinkling in their hands, to see what I was up to. Oh, a football game, how cute.

Our seats were in section 115, at the one-yard line, nine rows from the field. It was a crazy catty-corner angle from which to view a game. The field was almost at eye level. A team with the ball moving toward the opposite end zone slowly marched away. Years of watching at last educated the eye to accurately gauge the distances traveled through the jungle of moving legs and falling bodies. But oh, when a team had the ball marching toward my end zone, what a state of escalating urgency would fill the crowd! Our bodies could feel the collective thrill. If Charley Taylor, Paul Warfield, Art Monk, Bob Hayes, Jerry Rice, or Joe Morrison were running one of those tricky corner patterns, the ball would come rocketing skyward in my direction before the receiver ever made his break to the outside, seeming as though the pass were coming right to me. I could see the whites of their eyes as they looked for it coming in over their shoulders. I could hear the slap of the leather on their hands. I could hear the air leave their bodies as the players collided with one another, and then the ground.

The goal line was directly in front of me, and when a team was marching in close, and the defense would dig in, a goal line stand resounded with the thunderclap of pads and grunts and rebel yells.

I remember Jim Brown carrying Sam Huff on his back, and Tony Dorsett cutting so swiftly through the line that he would already be standing in the end zone while behemoth-sized linemen were still falling in upon one another like a collapsing house of cards. I saw Franco Harris, Larry Brown, Walter Payton, Tom Matte, Leroy Kelly, John Riggins, Emmitt Smith, and Gale Sayers do things that would make anyone with a sense of wonder stand and say, "Oh my god!" And that's what we said.

On a cold December afternoon, as the Redskins were making a push for the playoffs and the thrill of post-season possibilities lifted us poor success-starved fans into a state of high anxiety, O'Reilly had a change of heart. How he had come around to accept me as a person, he never did say, but he reached into his pocket, withdrew his flask, took a swig, and tapped me on the elbow with the back of his hand. Without saying a word, he handed me his flask of Irish whiskey.

Everyone in the row behind us, including his daughter and son-in-law, who had been watching us with concern for years, rejoiced.

For me, it was a personal triumph. From then on, I had a pal with whom to discuss the events on the field. Girlfriends complained that he and I wouldn't shut up the entire game.

We had a lot to talk about.

Older than me by thirty years, O'Reilly had listened to the exploits of Sammy Baugh on the radio. He followed Otto Graham, Sid Luckman, Cliff Battles, and Curly Lambeau. Together we watched as Fran Tarkenton, playing for the Giants, was sacked inside his five-yard line, right in front of us. Peevish as ever, he stood up and bounced the ball off the back of big defensive end Jimmy Jones's head. Diron Talbert, Manny Sistrunk, and Ron McDole, three members of the famed Over the Hill Gang, turned and pounced on him. Tarkenton was small, even for a quarterback. It wasn't pretty.

From that corner of the stadium, I saw Y. A. Tittle, Terry Bradshaw, Don Meredith, Johnny Unitas, Earl Morrall, Joe Montana, Billy Kilmer, Frank Ryan, Norman Snead, John Brodie, Phil Simms, Dan Marino, Randall Cunningham, Roman Gabriel, Brett Favre, Bart Starr, Ron Jaworski, and Joe Theismann.

Roger Staubach had perfect aim, perfect speed, perfect poise, perfect bloody everything. We hated him for being a Cowboy, and for being so damned perfect.

Sonny Jurgensen would get down on one knee in the huddle and pluck at the grass as he instructed his men, making up the play on the spot. As the play clock wound down, our hearts would leap into our throats. Is he going to Charley Taylor? Jerry Smith? Bobby Mitchell? You have to be damn good to make the Hall of Fame from a losing team. Those who saw Sonny play will never forget his marvelously unpredictable play-calling, the perfect spirals, his timing, the soft touch, accuracy, and his courage as he stood in and took a beating to deliver the ball. His limited play at the end of his career, his feud with Coach Allen, and his eventual retirement were sad events for us. And for the rest of our football lives, we would compare every quarterback thereafter to him. None of them measured up, not even close.

I remember that the air in the stadium smelled sweet with a mixture of hot chocolate, pipes, cigars, hot dogs, and beer, the perfect aromas for a football stadium. The team had a rowdy marching band dressed like Indian chiefs, and an equally rowdy group of barrel-chested male choral singers who wore burgundy blazers. Both inhabited one corner of the stadium and played their marches and sang their songs while swaying back and forth like a battalion of drunken Muppets. We listened through a tinny public address system and drowned them out as we sang along. Autumn twilight would dim the field and big lights atop the stadium would come on in stages, reflecting off the burgundy helmets, the sights and smells and sounds creating a sensual ambiance that lingers through time. The fall color NFL uniforms of dark mustard gold and burgundy, the other teams in white with hints of green or blue or silver, made the chill in the air warm with promise, and, as the clock ticked down and the sun faded and the temperature began to drop, so did the excitement heighten as season after season swelled, ebbed, crested, then slipped away. There were no TV screens in the stadium, and so every play was memorized by those in attendance. We would have to wait for the brief repeated highlights on the eleven o'clock news before bed that night.

When Robert F. Kennedy was murdered, it just made sense to rename the stadium for him. Though he wasn't a Washingtonian, he had certainly blazed a trail through the Capital City, and we understood that our town stood for something a lot bigger than local concerns. The stadium, after all, was geographically located on a straight line from the Capitol, the Washington Monument, and the Lincoln Memorial, taking what seemed its natural place among those glorious national landmarks.

Sometime in the 1970s, the number of VIPs on the sidelines began to obscure our view. Then came the mobile carts with TV cameras that went up and down the sidelines with the cameras and cameramen on accordion platforms that would rise and lower, blocking our view just when the game was coming our way. The working stiffs seated in the stands down low would throw whole cups of beer at them. Then one year, after the season's final game, when fans traditionally went onto the field to take down the home-side goal posts, they were unexpectedly met with helmeted police who savagely beat them with nightsticks. It was stunning and scary to witness up close.

We got the message. Things were changing in America, and the game experience was now shifting to favor the fans watching at home at the expense of the paying fans actually in attendance.

Get a couple of old RFK season ticket holders together and it's impossible not to open the lid on a hundred breathtaking moments. And why not? Sure it's sentimental, sure it's self-indulgent. But those indulgences are what make those pleasures so rich and enduring. These are moments we consider as much a part of our life and times as a child's graduation, a Thanksgiving family get-together, and ranked among the personal highs and lows of our lives.

For most Washington fans, you need only mention the names for the memories to rise up: Dick James, Billy Kilmer, Monte Coleman, Chris Hanburger, Rusty Tillman, Dexter Manley, Art Monk, Mark Mosely, Ray Knight, Len Hauss, Pat Fischer, Roy Jefferson, Bill Malinchak, Myron Potios, Jack Pardee, Paul Krause, Larry Brown, Gary Clark, Brig Owens, Doug Williams, Darrell Green, Kenny Houston. And, of course, there are the villains—Clint Longley and Lawrence Taylor. Longley, a quarterback replacement for the Cowboys, beat us on Thanksgiving Day with a hail mary at the end of the game. Walt Garrison was stopped at the one-yard line by Kenny Houston, a one-on-one tackle in the final seconds of the game, turning a potential tragedy into a never-forgotten triumph. Lawrence Taylor broke Joe Thiesmann's leg so brutally fans from all corners of the stadium claim to have heard it snap. Together we witnessed the dizzying success of the Gibbs Era and three Super Bowl triumphs. Other teams have won more, but those were ours.

We saw Sonny come in for one play, disobeying Coach Allen's orders to simply take a knee at the end of the half, and throw a forty-two-yard touchdown.

That play probably was a turning point in NFL history. When quarterbacks called the plays, everyone in the stands and at home would hold their breath, identifying with the man in the saddle, his style, his mind, the makeup of his character all factored in. But a corporate mentality was taking over in America, controlling everything from farming to football games. Jurgensen's play was for all intents and purposes the end of his career. A few years later, Joe Gibbs explained the seismic change in the game this way, "It's the coach who takes the blame for bad decisions, not the player. If I'm going to be

the one to get fired, then it's going to be me calling the plays."
It makes sense on a corporate basis, but not on a football one.
The person calling the plays is no longer the person whose
body is in danger. And once quarterbacks were no longer calling plays, they started getting hurt right and left. So the league
began changing rules to protect them, and inserted deep flaws
into the structure of what was, to me and those fans sitting
around me, for a time, a flawless game.

At a rainy Monday night football game, most of section 115
had gone home by the second half. O'Reilly said he wasn't feeling well, thought he'd leave, too. Before he did, he held out his
hand. I was startled by the unexpected formality. "I just want
you to know what a pleasure it's been sitting next to you and
talking all these years," he told me.

I arrived at the next game to find his seat empty. His daughter and son-in-law explained sadly that the Friday before that
Monday night game O'Reilly had gotten some bad news about
his health. He had walked out of the stadium at halftime and
stepped in front of a fast-moving bus.

I was the last person known to have seen him alive.

"It was like going to church," a friend and long-time Skins
devotee told me when the team moved out of RFK. "It meant
that much to people."

Now, those afternoons and evenings at RFK are just old
news. The highlights from those years look grainy and dark,
which is so odd when the memories are so vivid. The current
stadium the Redskins inhabit holds ninety thousand fans.
Contained therein are fifty-five thousand broken hearts. It
won't be long before we are gone as well.

In an interview with Darrell Green at the end of his career, I asked him if the players could feel the passion of the fans in the stands. He looked at me with wide-eyed incredulity. "You'd have to have been brain dead not to feel it. People talk all the time about Soldier Field in Chicago, or Lambeau Field in Green Bay. Trust me, they couldn't compare to what was going on in Washington, not even close!"

I'm glad the Redskins have moved on. It would be painful to see an advertisement slapped over the name of the place that holds so many myths, such legendary events. Thirty-six years of friends and football deserve better. Perhaps the team's mascot should change too. The Native North Americans I knew growing up during summers in rural Canada called themselves redskins. It was a mere distinction, like "white men." But the epithet "wahoo," that was a go as far as fighting for Native pride was concerned. But that's neither here nor there. The name "Redskins" is an antiquated throwback to a time of racial segregation and division that for some is still too painfully recent, and, once it's gone, will be an embarrassing memory. Plenty of other names would serve just as well. It is, after all, only a football team. Certainly, people matter more.

I don't go to the Redskins games anymore. Hey, nothing stays the same.

But every now and then, as football season returns, I look up from the sports pages to find myself still sitting in old RFK, section 115, row 9, seat number 2, gabbing with O'Reilly, and still missing Sonny.

I Study the Crowds

I've always been fascinated by the myriad faces and types of humanity that populate the human zoo. And in America, there is no better place to study our particular version of the human animal than at a baseball game. Unlike other sports, all manner of Americans can, and do, love baseball. To me, the term National Pastime has never meant the most popular sport in the nation, although for a long time it was, and, truth be told, may still well be. Instead, I always felt it meant that the best way to candidly observe an American in his and her most natural habitat is when passing time at a baseball game.

I Look at the Pictures

The photographs of the fans in the stands go all the way back to Civil War America. The pictures open a window to another universe, a lost world to which it may seem a personal connection simply isn't possible. It *is* possible, however, and those old photos provide the formula for making that connection real. We are all—them, us, then, now—watching the game.

As I scan the crowds, the men wearing hats, coats, and ties, the women in hats, too, and dresses covering them up to the neck, it is not difficult to effect a Ted Turner–style colorization in my mind, to insert the sound of hubbub and spontaneous roar. I know the grass was green, the sky was blue. I hear the crack of the bat, the slap and pop of leather. I see the attitude of the times in their faces—defiance, cockiness, worry; a studied personal posture on public display. They were fighting the Great Depression, or worrying about loved ones at war, or basking in peacetime pleasures, all of this held in a momentary stasis, suspended, as they turned their attention to another kind of problem solving, but always with one consistent theme: doing a job. That's how we talk about a baseball player's responsibility. He does his job. This isn't romance. It's a way of looking at the world. Three strikes and you're out. He got there first. He gets to walk. He hit it out of the park. Keep it in front of you. Hit the cut-off man. Keep your eye on the ball. Don't make an error. You're either safe, or you're out. At games they are all there, the elements to be successful. The way to do a job.

I Go To The Games

So did others, from the very first, by the tens of thousands. A century and a half, or about two-thirds of our country's history up to now, is wrapped up in this shared experience. Before there were bleachers, people climbed fences, sat on hillsides, stood just beyond the field of play, forming a human perimeter where future outfield fences would one day stand. They climbed trees and sat in the branches like flocks of fedora-wearing birds. At one time, the game must have seemed as new as the country itself. Grandstands had to be constructed. Entrance fees needed to be charged to make the events sustainable. Why did they come? To see local boys make good, to pit one neighborhood or town against another, for civic pride. The game is the curiosity-seeker's perfect thrill; spectacle conjured from the available elements of open air, open field, wit, and brawn. Wait one more pitch, and just see what happens.

Over time, fans made social and political statements, first with their posture, then, later on, with their appearance. From cocky to colorful. Wealthy or working class. Anti-war or conservative. Socially flamboyant. Posturing or unselfconscious. Patriotic. Contemporary. And, at long last, casual. Fan behavior has run the gamut, from stoic observance to complete rapture, to pandemonium, flooding the streets after Bobby Thompson's "Shot Heard 'Round the World," or following the home run king around the bases. Even when away from the game, it is somehow comforting to realize that the game is always being played, as long as the weather is warm and the evenings are long.

Other sports claim to make history. Baseball actually does make history. Whether breaking the color barrier or canceling the World Series to solve a labor dispute, or shamefully allowing an All-Star game to end without a victor at a time when the country itself was enforcing only the laws a privileged elite deemed necessary, baseball runs its parallel course with the struggles of America.

Better sportswriters than I—Red Smith, David Halberstam, Thomas Boswell, Bill James—have chronicled the sport's inner connection with the American temperament. Like them, at some games I feel the eerie attendance of many generations. At other times, I sense a strange missing element—those fans who have moved on.

Like fans, certain players look as if they could only have existed in the time in which they played. Take Jacob "Old Eagle Eye" Beckley, for instance, who, to this day, holds the record for first basemen, with 25,000 chances. Most putouts, 23,696, most games played, 2,368. He played for Pittsburgh, Cincinnati, and St. Louis. He made 2,930 hits and batted .309 for his career. After twenty years in the big leagues, he retired in 1907. Even his nickname seems antique.

But look at John "Happy Jack" Chesbro. Where Beckley looks as though he could only have lived at the turn of the last century, "Happy Jack" looks as though he might be the guy sitting beside you, or stepping through security next to you, at a game today. He won forty-one games in 1904.

Many of the platitudes you hear about the game of baseball are true. For Americans, it *is* a timeless game. This is more than a play on words because the game is not governed by a clock counting down the minutes until the end. Its timelessness rests in the fact that the game and its history can connect generations and maybe even epochs of culture with its long, woven rope of happenstance. It is true, as well, that power and greed can corrupt and ruin the game. But isn't it ever thus? In 1911, Walter Johnson, baseball's greatest pitcher, wrote in *Baseball Magazine* of what he called "The Great American Principle of Dog Eat Dog," and he wasn't talking about ballpark franks.

My point is that baseball has always been popular. Consequently, it has always attracted large crowds. Large crowds attract money, gamblers, wheeler dealers, and confidence men. It's astonishing how similar today's baseball issues are to those that have arisen over the last 150 years.

On Opening Day 2003, the *New York Times* pointed out that from 1901 to 1994, ten men hit fifty or more homers in a season eighteen times. From 1995 to 2002, the *Times* went on to remind us, ten men also hit fifty or more home runs in a season eighteen times. What once took ninety-three years to accomplish now takes seven. Clearly, something has changed. Is there a Watergate waiting to happen over juiced balls and TV money? Power and greed can corrupt and ruin anything, maybe everything. But they don't have to.

Our culture and its custodians should take care to not despoil such a well-made thing as baseball.

The game, whether played by anonymous souls whose names we'll never know, or the big-money-making star athletes we've become so suspicious of, may be such a part of who we are that even the clown princes of America can't screw it up for very long. Just teach your kids to play, and the tradition will survive. And if it survives, perhaps those things that could heal baseball's problems—doing your job, making a sacrifice—might just heal some of America's problems, too.

Meanwhile, look at the pictures of the crowds. I'm that little speck of color in the upper deck, and happy to have a seat there, right where I belong.

The Mayor of 417

"Old School!" the young man shouted.

His voice came from the middle of the crowd as we herded toward the escalator at the F Street Metro after a Washington Capitals hockey game. It took me a second to realize he was shouting at me. He and his pals were reacting to my classic white, star-spangled Dale Hunter hockey sweater—and, I assume, my gray hair—as he called out again, "Old School, man!"

You would have loved this guy, and his friends—early twenties, beefy, unkempt, a bunch of ragtag rabble-rousers for sure. The speaker was wearing baggy shorts despite the cold winter night, a floppy knitted cap with a ball hanging from the top on a thread, and a New School Caps sweater in black. It took me a second to remember that I'm fifty years old, and yes, looking more and more grizzled myself these days.

I turned. Everyone moving along between the young men and myself was expecting a reply; everyone seemed to be somewhere in age between his and mine. So I said, "Every school is 'Old School' sooner or later, my friend." The words rolled off my tongue, and the crowd had a chuckle. But as I made my way home that night, I thought, "When the hell did I become Old School?" and even more importantly, "Is that a good thing?"

My personal confrontations with mortality aside, it's kind of nice to hear a bunch of young turks laying out some props for anything called "Old School." I've spilled a lot of ink attempting to connect what has been good and memorable in my forty-plus years of being a sports fan with what we experience as fans today. The evolving relationships between fans and the sports they follow, and the changes in the games brought about by design or default, are all grist for my mill.

One thing I know for sure: I can't be a couch potato sports fan. I've got to go to the games.

Contrary to popular wisdom, I don't think football is perfect for television. On TV, you can't see the secondary fan out as the receivers penetrate the zones, while simultaneously the pocket forms, as the defensive linemen battle their way to the quarterback. When you're there, you can take in the whole play, which is happening all at once—not the little bits and pieces, albeit beautifully laid out and directed, that the play becomes on television, repeated again and again in its various elements. The crisp air outside, the mood of the crowd, the simple challenge of getting to the stadium—these are all part of football for me.

I feel the same way about the other sports I follow. A high towering fly ball arching up and into a summer sky will get oohs and aaahs from a crowd even when they know it's an easy out. No camera can capture that in the same way that human eyes can from the stands. In hockey, a turnover at the blue line will cause the players to peel back all at once, like a school of fish all changing direction at the same instant. You won't see that on TV. Perhaps basketball can be caught all at once on camera. But the bouncing ball, the squeak of shoes on wood, the yip and yak of the players, and the slapping of flesh all make more sense in person.

In the late 1950s, when my father first took me to games, he wouldn't let me duck under the turnstiles. He would stop me and make me turn the metal arm, and once inside, he'd have me check the counter that registered the number of people who had passed through. The following day, he'd show me the page in the newspaper where game attendance was reported.

"If you hadn't been there, that number would be different," he'd say. He wanted me to realize that my being there mattered. I believed him, and I still do.

My father always had a cordial word for the ticket-taker, and would hold up the line to get in, waiting for a cordial reply. Once at our seats, he wouldn't sit down until he had formally greeted all the familiar folk around us, shaking hands as he inquired about their health and that of their loved ones, and receiving a prognosis for the outcome of the day's contest.

I hadn't realized the power of his example until last season, when, while I was tailgating at a Redskins game, a woman I didn't recognize approached me.

"Are you a Caps season ticketholder?" she asked.

"Yes."

"In section 417?"

"Yes."

"Well," she laughed, "my friends and I sit a dozen rows behind you. Every game we watch you arrive and shake everyone's hand. We call you 'The Mayor of 417.' We think it's good luck to watch you make your entrance! On nights when you don't show up, we worry. It's good to see you here, too!"

The bonds that exist in my section at Caps games evolved spontaneously. Scattered about the first few rows in the upper deck by the rail at center ice, we have gravitated together, closing ranks against the opposition fans who sometimes clog the sections. Washington, D.C., being the Capital of the Empire, boasts two congressional delegations from each state of the union; when joined with the Canadian Embassy and that country's presence here in the Capital City, representation in significant numbers for virtually every opposing team is guaranteed. That, plus the fact that D.C. is a bus, car, or train ride from Philly, New Jersey, New York City, and Pittsburgh, means that from time to time an infestation can occur. Measures must be taken. We frown upon section dwellers who give tickets to opposing fans. We keep an eye on seats as they come open and hurry to recommend replacements. We monitor each other's "rage" during more heated engagements to ensure a proper level of enthusiasm is maintained. We worry when one of us is absent, and make inquiries. We have a regular Irish pub a block away we adjourn to for heady analyses, breakdowns, and, in my case, meltdowns!

In front of me sits the Irish Barrister of 417, ready with answers to legal questions and points of hockey law as far as history and the rule book are concerned. He keeps a cool head unless his native Boston Bruins are in town, whereupon he turns traitor, dons his hometown's sweater, and advocates against us. His wife has become the Conscience of 417, ruling on what behavior is and is not tolerated in our section. She is patient, understanding even, but her patience has its limits. They have suffered sitting in front of me, getting doused with popcorn and the occasional spritzing of beer, and my ber-serker insistence on theories and histories which are proven time and again to be dead wrong. I scream and yell, "My name is Ulf Dahlén, I just flew in from Düsseldorf, and boy are my arms tired!" They must constantly remind me that Ulf Dahlén is not from Düsseldorf, which is in Germany. Dahlén is from Östersund, Sweden. No matter. I have accused these nice people of toilet-papering my house and threatened to whip out my American Express card and join them on vaca-tions to Ireland. And they've had to endure a litany of horrid cheers I've made up for nearly every player, inspiring my son to scold on more than one occasion, "Nobody makes up their own cheers, Dad!" *Au contraire, mon frère!*

The Italian Brothers who sit to my left carry the rage of our section. One is a lawyer and the other a software designer, and the wit and bile that they bring to be meted out to opponents, refs, owners, and sometimes even our own players, can inspire the entire section with a rebel zeal that is hard to imitate out-side the building. There's the Jewish Mother of 417, ever seek-ing the proper wealthy Jewish athlete to marry her daughter. On Meet the Players Night for season ticket-holders, she will leave a note in a Jewish player's locker to that effect. Her son names his fantasy teams "The Mighty Hebes," and Dad, a der-matologist by day, collects jerseys from Jewish players from all sports.

The Grande Dame of 417 sits behind me. Her husband, a veteran fighter pilot who flew P-51 Mustangs in WWII and used to attend every game with her, passed away a few years ago. But she still comes to most games and cheers louder than anyone. "C'mon guys!" she'll scream into the back of my head. Her groans when things go poorly are so full of genuine pain we sometimes turn to see if she's all right, only to be met with a scowl that evaporates into a loving please-forgive-me smile before she resumes her admonitions to play better. She has banned the word "sucks" from the section, and although we are all in agreement with her edict, it can be a hard rule to enforce, especially during the playoffs, and on those rare nights she isn't there, we feel compelled to scold one another should that standard be broken in her absence.

We have the Rainbow Fascist, the Quiet Men, the Blonde Bombshell, and last of all, the Sage of 417, who, having retired from season ticketland after two decades, no longer sits with us regularly, but still pays his old section a visit when he does attend a game.

Attending all forty-one games in a season can be a challenge, and I have on occasion been pinned with the title Partial Plan Patterson, my mayoral status called up for review if skipping games threatens to become a habit.

It's a community that sprang to life around a number, a box of seats in the upper nosebleeds where the "real fans" congregate. We aren't there to see and be seen; we're actually there to watch the games, and we live and die with each contest. "Welcome to 417," someone will say when a stranger appears, nudging his or her way to a seat holding a tray of food and drinks. Chances are, we won't be strangers for long.

Forty years of watching sports in person bring me here, standing on a Metro platform, half tipsy, after a game. A young man and his rowdy cohorts come blustering through the crowd. "Old School!" he shouts again, seeing me for the second time, and as he and his friends file past, each one of them shakes my hand.

The Nearest Thing to Perfection

My mother, rest her soul, used to hear sports prognosticators on the TV or radio and click her teeth in disgust. "Everyone," she would smirk, "thinks they can do two things better than anyone else. Run a restaurant and manage a baseball team."

She loved only one sport, baseball. Football was just "a bunch of silly overgrown fat men falling all over each other." Basketball was "freakishly tall men jumping up and down with their hands in the air." Hockey? She would sigh, stare out the window for a moment, and then mutter something about Bobby Orr.

Like all true fans, she was passionate about the sport she loved. When I say love, I mean it in its truest, most irrational, devotional form. She believed her team would win the World

Series every year, no matter what the stats, no matter what the record. And when they didn't, she felt betrayed, heartbroken, and angry. "That's it!" she would harrumph after the last game of every season her team didn't win the pennant, "I'm never watching another baseball game! Ever!"

"Aw, c'mon, Mom," I would laugh, "you know you'll be back next year."

"No, I won't! You mark my words, Jimmy Patterson, never again!"

My mother was a good Christian woman from a small prairie town, and she had what some might think of as rather peculiar notions. "How can you call them the Washington Senators," she would ask in perfect innocence, "when there's not a single one of them from Washington?" She grew up watching hometown boys play ball, and didn't understand why local origins weren't a prerequisite for playing in the Big Leagues. "Wouldn't that make more sense?" she'd say. "Then the town would really get behind them, and there wouldn't be so many empty seats." The second time the Senators left town, I began to think that she might be onto something. Of course, she blamed it all on the Yankees. If you were really good, you ended up in New York, and there was nothing anyone could do about it. That's America.

Opening Day was her big thing. Starting fresh and all of that. She would write me a note to get me out of school saying I had a doctor's appointment and take me to the game her-self. Getting a chance to see the President throw out the first ball superseded any moral qualms she might have had about lying to the nuns over where I was going to be that afternoon. She wanted me to be able to say I saw Eisenhower, Kennedy, Johnson, and Nixon. I saw them and I'm glad.

But her moral balance had an uneven keel. She didn't understand how you could call it a strike if the batter didn't swing. She could not abide base stealing, and would boo even if the home team stole a base. When diehard fans would turn and look questioningly at her, she would scold, "Stealing is wrong, young man. It doesn't matter who does it, and it doesn't matter why." They loved her for her quirkiness. I know I sure did. Not being from D.C., she felt no overriding obligation to root for the home team throughout the season, though she thought it rude to go to a game and root for the opposition. So she picked teams with players she could admire to root for from home. The Pittsburgh Pirates with Roberto Clemente and Bob Gibson's St. Louis Cardinals were her loves when I was growing up. When, in 1966, the World Series came to Baltimore, she had my father scalp tickets because, you never know, you might not get this close again. She took me then, too, and she was right. I have not been able to make it back yet to a World Series game.

Growing up in the Depression, she was unable to attend college, but she loved to read. Every now and again, she would drop a *New Yorker* magazine into my lap, or some reprint of the writings of Red Smith. "Ninety feet between the bases is the nearest thing to perfection that man has yet achieved," he wrote, and, "Baseball is dull, only to dull minds."

My mother loved crowds, she loved spectacle, and she loved the idea of seeing history made. She would scream and whoop and cry and get so excited she'd want to burst. I'll never know what she would have thought of the Bud Selig era—the cancellation of the World Series in '94, the All-Star Game of 2002, the controversies over the juiced ball and the shrunken strike zone, the spiraling salaries, high ticket prices, and falling historical records, all of which, I have told myself, kept me sitting out the seasons since her passing.

My guess is that our conversation over these issues would have been a short one. Then she would have wrinkled her brows, her brown eyes would have grown darker still, and with a clenched fist and a stiff lower lip, she would have said loud and clear, as she did every Opening Day year after year, "Play ball!"

The Myth of the Casual Fan

All sports need their Die-Hard Fans, no exceptions. Over the course of an average Die-Hard Fan's fandom, he or she could be personally accountable for bringing hundreds, if not thousands, of "casual fans" to a sport. Creating converts, if you will.

As for myself, when I look back at the last thirty years of attending games of all kinds, I actually have a difficult time putting a round number to the amount of first-timers I have dragged to sporting events great and small. The number is huge, I can assure you. And this number doesn't include the casual fans I have invited to my home for World Series, Super Bowl, Stanley Cup, World Cup, or simply Big Game parties. At those gatherings, real fans were forged and a lifetime involvement with sports begun. One of the greatest joys of fandom is turning on a friend to a sport—recruiting, training, explaining, educating. There's nothing quite like the enjoyment of sharing the fan experience with someone for whom it is a new thing. I don't know a single Die-Hard Fan who doesn't have similar stories to tell.

What is a casual fan?

Well, here in the real world, casual fans are ones who aren't fanatical, but nonetheless keep their eye on a particular sport, and when a team or player that excites them comes to town, or their favorite team is playing well, or a friend shows up with tickets, they are more than ready to jump in and go see a game. Such a fan might even own a team cap or jersey, sported whenever the time is right. And that's as it should be.

But corporations that have taken on the business of selling sports have a rather different view of the casual fan. It's becoming obvious that the networks, as well as their copycats in the lower media, are most interested, not in the kind of casual fan described above, brought into the game on a personal, one-on-one basis, but in a mass audience of what would more appropriately be termed "window shoppers."

So it's got to hurt Die-Hards like me, who have spent a lifetime bringing new fans to the sports we love, when a big media mouthpiece like Fox TV's Pam Oliver explains the current network dogma pertaining to fans. Responding to the bickering that ensued during the 2002 NFL season when, reporting from the sidelines during a Packers vs. Bears game, she told her viewers about a brouhaha between a Bears defenseman and the Bears offensive coordinator. Oliver explained that the network feels the presence of "reporters" like herself on the sidelines is necessary to keep the interest of casual fans. Speaking on ESPN's *Mike & Mike in the Morning* radio show, she went on to explain what TV talking heads have been telling us for years—that since Die-Hard Fans will watch anyway, the money for the networks is in the casual fan. Make the games appealing to the channel-hopping bandwagoner, this myth states, and you can realize extra ratings, higher ad revenues, and a larger market share.

Sounds smart, doesn't it? But there are a few glaring flaws in that argument. First off, the games aren't "covered" by reporters. They're "brought" to you by the networks and other media in partnership with the leagues. No real, self-respecting journalist can claim any professional objectivity or integrity when his or her employer is partnered with the entity being covered.

Second, what Oliver calls casual fans are actually only curiosity-seekers, novelty hounds. They're peering at something they don't really intend to buy (into). Like window shoppers, as soon as they find something better to do, they're out of here.

But what the three-headed beast of Sports League, Sports Union, and Sports Media is doing is relentlessly tweaking the rules and remaking the games to appeal to these window shoppers, who don't really care in the first place, by freighting the rules in favor of offense and sensational plays and neutering defenses, by altering the outcome of games by some unseen and unnamed judge *up in the booth*, during the last two minutes of each half. And where does that leave your regular customer, the Die-Hard Fan who'll (presumably) always be there? What does it do to your product? And how badly are you taking your customers for granted?

Let's pick on the NFL some more. As of this writing each and every team—thirty-two and counting—gets more than a hundred million dollars per year from network television for the right to bring you the games. Not surprisingly, all of that money is claimed by the players' union under the logic that people tune in to watch players play the game. I would suggest that is only partially true. Most of the Die-Hard Fans I know tune in to see their team. The players come and go, but loyalty to the *team* trumps loyalty to a player in all but the most special circumstances.

Also, since revenue from the ticket-buying public is now far down the list of NFL revenues, fan satisfaction is a low priority when it comes to rules changes and game-altering decision making. And none of that network cash is passed on to fans in the form of lower prices.

Another startling fact is that the networks lose lots of money on the NFL. The networks rationalize the expense by claiming that they use the high ratings for the games to promote their weekly entertainment line-ups. Watch and you will notice that the premier advertising slots during NFL contests are reserved for in-house network adverts for the shows they are currently promoting. What effect this has on actual programming during non-sports-related broadcasts is hard to tell. One of these days some sharp CPA is going to stand up at a finance meeting and suggest that the NFL has become so dependent on television that the networks could actually pay the league whatever they please: where else can the league go? On that day the NFL will rediscover the fan in the stands, currently just a television extra who is paying good money for the privilege.

The NHL is different. It's the last professional league that still depends on the fan at the gate for the bulk of its revenue. Therefore, the spectacle at the arena is still aimed primarily at the fan in the stands rather than the fan on the couch. NHL owners, traditionally, won't even sacrifice seats for better TV camera vantage points. This makes the big shift the NHL has made—away from fighting and toward a more sophisticated on-ice product—all the more courageous. Also, it means that the league has had to adapt to the changing demographic taking place in the stands: more upscale as ticket prices soar, more educated, and more sensitive to the violence that was considered a necessary part of the game in earlier eras.

We hear all the time that greed has taken over the big leagues these days, and it's hard to argue against that view. And maybe the suits are right. Maybe the Die-Hard Fan like myself is antiquated, obsolete, a thing of the past. Maybe the Unholy Trinity of Players' Unions, Big Media, and Ownership has created a marketing combine so sophisticated that it can keep the window shoppers turning over in such numbers and with such constancy that those things we used to value about sports—the traditions, the values, and the memories from one generation to the next—no longer matter to the health of the business. With corporate naming rights, it's figured out how to get advertisements into the body and content of "news" stories, both print and broadcast media, with nary a peep of protest from the lap dogs in the sporting press.

Perhaps, by abandoning the Die-Hard Fan, the suits are telling us that they don't even care about their own survival so long as there's a big payoff now, and for as long as they can make it last. When the house of cards falls, they'll take their profits and leave our games in a state of ruin.

But make no mistake, it's the Die-Hard Fans who keep the games alive. They're the ones who buy the tickets, who watch and listen to the media broadcasts of the games, who follow

the boxes in the papers, who purchase gear, and, most importantly, who get their friends, the true casual fans, to start going
to the games.

Walter Johnson: Baseball's Big Train

(a book review)

How do you like a baseball book that begins with post–Civil War border clashes between Kansas and Missouri, with renegade Confederate cavalry remnants terrorizing the countryside, with Cole Younger and the guerilla gangs of William Quantrill and "Bloody Bill" Anderson?

When Walter Johnson's mother was just eight years old, two men asked for her father's permission to sleep in his barn. He stayed up all night to make sure they didn't steal his horses. While her mother cooked breakfast the next morning, the two strangers sat on the porch and regaled the little girl with stories. One even whipped out a pistol and took down a blue jay with a single shot. Later that day, a sheriff's posse rode up and informed them that their visitors had been none other than Frank and Jesse James.

From the lawless Great Plains to the oilfields of southern California at Olinda, America's second gold rush, a narrative begins to weave its way, for baseball is old enough and geographically broad enough to be storied in parallel lines with the making of America. They called it "town ball" back then, at the turn of the last century, when, on weekends, the men of one town would challenge the men of another to a game. Local bands would play, there would be cookouts, special trains would roll between the competing municipalities, and, certainly, there would be lots and lots of gambling.

Everywhere Walter Johnson played baseball in those early years of the twentieth century, he was legend. They called him "The Big Swede," though he had no Swedish ancestry, but he was so fair, so big and strong, he challenged everyone's frame of reference. As his legend grew, it became known that his size and strength and toughness of spirit were only matched by his gentleness and consideration for smaller, weaker mortals.

It didn't take long for him to gain notoriety in a sport endlessly seeking talent. He worked his way from the coastal leagues in California to the big time in just three years. Word reached Joe Cantillon of the Washington Nationals Baseball Club about a pitcher in the Idaho State League who mowed down 166 batters in eleven games and pitched seventy-seven consecutive scoreless innings. The scouting report comes down to us, "This boy throws so fast you can't see'm…and he knows where he's throwing the ball because if he didn't there would be dead bodies strewn all over Idaho."

Later, the pitcher's wife would keep scrapbooks, meticulously preserving the precious artifacts of the man's life and career, the man whose arrival in the nation's capital had been so anticipated he was nicknamed by the press "Big Train" for the big train everyone was waiting on that would carry the Nationals' new phenom into town. The year was 1907, and he was still mowing down hitters for the hometown Nats when they won the World Series in 1924.

Sixty-five years later, his daughter's son, a grown man, would pull those massive albums of clippings and press releases, photographs and family memorabilia down from their glass cases, and be awed by the story pieced together from those fragmentary artifacts collected along life's way.

We have that grandson, Henry (Hank) W. Thomas, to thank for the incredible story of *Walter Johnson: Baseball's Big Train*.

Now fifty-eight years old, Hank Thomas stands in the beer garden at the ballpark in Hagerstown, Maryland, cracking peanuts, sipping beer, and talking baseball. Watching a baseball game with Hank Thomas is a unique experience. He chats amiably about politics, history, and music, tossing in a random appreciation of the odd skirt floating by, and certainly he talks about times past and present in the great game of baseball. And when I say past, I don't just mean over the course of his own lifetime, but three lifetimes and more. He articulates the word itself with a certain reverence, like you might hear an artist use the word "painting," with the emphasis on the consonant in the middle of the word: "Baseball."

During a game, you notice that Hank Thomas has developed a sixth sense for baseball's crucial moments. He looks up when he hears something in the crack of the bat, his beak of a nose up in the wind like some nearly extinct bird of the game, hawking the air, hovering. He knows exactly where to look to catch up with the play in progress so as not to miss a critical moment, then returns to the thought he was developing, finding it right where he left off.

Being with him at a ballpark, you get the feeling that he has seen ten thousand games. And he has. In his book, he relives the games of yesteryear as though he were present with them in time. Writing the book about his grandfather, tearing into thousands of box scores, recreating ecstatic moments until now only preserved in those tiny fossilized boxes of little numbers, has plunged him into a matrix world of baseball's deepest delights. It is so easy to follow him there. He long ago stopped worrying about who was playing, who was winning; he doesn't keep score, meaning he doesn't score the game, except in his head. Hank just wants to see good baseball, and he doesn't care about the league, the team, or the venue.

He can't remember when he last paid to see a big league game. Since the Senators left his hometown, Washington, D.C., way back in 1971, he spent the intervening years until the big game's return attending minor pro league games, professional league games, and wherever organized baseball is played. He wants to be where the beer is cheap and the peanuts are salty. He even general-managed Bethesda's Big Train, named after his grandfather, their first year in the Clark Griffith League, a league of NCAA baseball prospects that plays a forty-game season in midsummer between spring and fall semesters. It's great baseball.

Want to know what Hank has to say about being a GM? "It was terrible! It turned baseball into work! I want to *enjoy* the game, not suffer through it like it's some kinda job!"

Walter Johnson was terrified that his amazing fastball would one day kill a man, so he rarely threw inside. When the great Ty Cobb realized this, he started to crowd the plate. He got more hits off Johnson that way than anybody else. Others weren't so brave. Cobb remembered it this way, "The first time I faced him I watched him take that easy wind-up—and then something went past me that made me flinch. I hardly saw the pitch, but I heard it. The thing just hissed with danger. Every one of us knew we'd met the most powerful arm ever turned loose in a ballpark."

Will Rogers speculated that if Johnson had played for the mighty New York Giants he most likely would not have lost a single game in eighteen years.

Thomas's biography of his grandfather is pure baseball beginning to end. Unlike other baseball classics—like Roger Kahn's *The Boys of Summer*, dripping with nostalgia and ripe with sublime social commentary, or Thomas Boswell's *How Life Imitates the World Series*, which is a baseball voyage of discovery with the 1979 Baltimore Orioles, both must-reads—Thomas's book is history told from inside the lines, and, as any good history book should be, is packed with sources: sixty-nine pages of footnotes, a ten-page bibliography, a comprehensive index, fourteen pages of the great pitcher's stats, and pages and pages of personal game-day photographs from the family collection.

"The publishers and even the printers thought I was crazy to insist on so many pictures, but they help bring the story back to life," he insists, and he's right. Best of all, Walter Johnson arrives in D.C. on page 37. No foolin' around with preliminaries, we get right to the games. From there we are treated to a history rich and wide, and tons of baseball.

When Clark Griffith managed the Nationals, if there wasn't a pennant on the line—and more often than not, there wasn't—the last home game of the season would be a "joke game." Fans loved it. Outfielders were called gardeners. The right gardener would perch up on the Bull Durham sign, swinging his legs, or roam around the infield completely out of position. Johnson played in center during joke games, but when called in to pitch an inning or two to please the crowd, he would lob balls at the plate allowing hitters to spray them around the park, returning to his position in center in mock disgrace.

"Just think," Thomas says, "without those joke games shaving off mere fractions from Johnson's lifetime statistics, he has records that nobody would ever have broken!" In 1913, for instance, Johnson's ERA for the season was an incredible 1.09, but with the joke game stats added in, his ERA for the year ballooned to 1.14, surrendering the All-Time Single Season ERA record to the Cardinals Bob Gibson in 1968, at 1.12.

It was in one of those joke games that Babe Ruth got his first big league hit.

Thomas argues that 1913 was most likely the best season ever for a big league pitcher. Johnson won thirty-six games and lost seven. He led the league in wins, winning percentage (.837) ERA, complete games (29), innings (346), strikeouts (243), and walked only 38. He also led the league in shutouts (11). Batters averaged .187 against him. He batted .266 with a slugging percentage of .433. Twenty-eight of his wins were by two runs or less and he was 20-3 on the road. Not too shabby. He handled all 103 of his chances without committing an error. This fielding accomplishment was the best by a pitcher in both leagues until 1976, and still stands in the American League today.

The numbers don't tell the human story. In these pages, black-and-white two-dimensional figures suddenly morph back into full color and three dimensions, like in a James Cameron film. Calvin Coolidge and John McGraw, Will Rogers and Lou Gehrig, Sam Rice and Joe Jackson, Grantland Rice and Shirley Povich become living, breathing men living big lives with big things on the line. It is their world, and through Hank Thomas's steady lens we can see, hear, and get a feel for their time, their passions, and their struggles with fate. Johnson's duels with Cobb, his relationship with Griffith, the endless road trips, the exhibition games around the country before and after each season, and, as today, the bickering with management over money, fill out the picture in very real terms.

Writing in the July 1911 issue of *Baseball Magazine*, Johnson described the relationship between player and management this way, "(It's) the Great American Principle of Dog Eat Dog...the employer tries to starve out the laborer, and the laborer tries to ruin the employer's business. They quarrel over a bone and try to rend each other like coyotes." Benjamin Minor, the Nationals' president, once reacted to Johnson's request for a raise by telling Clark Griffith, "Johnson had a bad season this year, he only won twenty-eight games."

It was Walter Johnson who handed the Yankees their first defeat in their new home, Yankee Stadium.

Walter Johnson won 417 games in his big league career. The legendary Bob Feller speculated in his autobiography that, if Johnson had been allowed to change teams, he could easily have won another hundred. He still holds twenty-eight major league records, thirty-nine American League records.

Hank Thomas wrote this marvelous book over a five-year period in the late 1980s–early 1990s. He couldn't have known that he would eerily foreshadow the events of the late 1990s, after labor strife caused the cancellation of the World Series, with his description of the aftermath of the Black Sox scandal of 1920. Thomas unwittingly unearths Major League Baseball's remedy for fan desertion—juice the ball, bring in the fences, and shrink the strike zone. Sure enough, as they did in the late 1990s and early 2000s, homers soared, records fell, and diehards screamed, "This isn't baseball!" Sound familiar? The only thing missing was steroids.

Today, Hank Thomas runs a baseball memorabilia business called Phenom Sports. When asked if he plans to write another book he says, "God no! If you want another book, YOU write it!" And after a few deep breaths, he adds, "I've done two great things in my life. I wrote the book about my grandfather, and I made the audio record of baseball's early greats [*The Glory of Their Time*, with Lawrence S. Ritter]. You know, most people don't even get to do one great thing. I've done two."

Every season, when the robins and the cherry blossoms return to Washington, D.C., I try to get jazzed up for the baseball season ahead by picking up a baseball book I haven't read. There are always plenty to choose from, but none better than *Walter Johnson: Baseball's Big Train* the definitive history of a man, an era, and a game of games.

I Am a 9-10er

As an American and a lover of freedom and the processes of a free society, the events of Tuesday, September 11, 2001, have filled me with the same grief, outrage, loathing, and lust for vengeance as they have so many millions at home and throughout what we have referred to for decades as "The Free World."

I was eleven years old when President Kennedy was murdered. I can remember how that apocalyptic event, coming as it did not long after the Cuban Missile Crisis, plunged our society into an abyss of uncertainty, fear, and dread. And we were a people already suffering from the prospect of Mutual Assured Destruction and the many lethal concepts that the realities of the Cold War inflicted on the American psyche.

It is hard to describe the mindset all of us—even kids—carried throughout our daily routine. Growing up in Washington, D.C., I can remember very well looking up into the sky and imagining the bomb burst that would end all our lives, our civilization, our planetary existence. These anxieties were compounded over the years, not only by the uncertainties of the Cold War, but by the frustration of the seemingly unending conflict in Vietnam, which divided families, sapped our nation's wealth and credit, sparked inflation, and took from us so many friends, both warriors and draft resisters. And the terrifying and inexplicable assassinations continued.

Cynicism crept into the American political mindset, and it has lived there ever since.

And then, as so often happens in times of peace, a new naiveté set in. Perhaps it was a result of the collapse of the Soviet Union and the sense of relief that the Cold War was at last over. Perhaps the legacy of Pearl Harbor—that America's military would never again stand down as it did after World War I—led us also to believe that there were certain constants in the nature of international evil that required us as a nation to be forever ready to fight a world war at a moment's notice.

Now it seems we have been given yet another shocking lesson about the realities of our world.

As a publisher, and a believer in and upholder of our various hard-won freedoms, including freedom of speech and the right of assembly, and of the right of the people to be secure in their persons, houses, and papers, I am as frightened by politicians suggesting that we must now abbreviate those freedoms in order to cope with a world gone wrong at the hands of terrorists, as I am by the potential deeds of the terrorists themselves.

Could they speak to us now, would the lost soldiers of D-Day, Argonne Woods, Gettysburg, or Valley Forge tolerate such a notion?

I am also chagrined at the idea that for America now, in the aftermath of this terrible act of war, "everything has changed." All I can say to that is, not for me.

For most of the weekend of November 22, 1963, my family stayed home, watched the horrible news broadcasts surrounding Kennedy's death, and made a thousand cookies, with, as my mother remembered it, "a tear in every one."

But on Sunday, November 24, 1963, my family took a few hours off from the horrible realities of the hour and watched the Washington Redskins play the Philadelphia Eagles in Philadelphia. It may seem distant and strange now, but a semblance of normalcy mattered to us then as we faced so much uncertainty each new day would bring thereafter. We didn't know then if we were truly on the brink of another world war.

The NFL has stated since that it regrets not canceling the games that day. But on November 24, it meant a lot to us to see our team play. Yes, it was a somber event. But there was comfort for us in watching our team, in seeing the grief, fear, and uncertainty in the eyes of strangers—who really weren't strangers anymore. They were Americans, like us, who loved and were grieving for their country.

I didn't know anyone who thought the NFL should not have played. We needed to carry on, and to be assured that our world had not changed, to see life go on as usual in spite of tragedy.

We needed that then. I think we need it now.

I think the NFL should have played this weekend, and show the world that although things may be different, *nothing has changed.*

Pierian Dreams

The Conversation
We Are Born Into

I am *The Reluctant Scholar.* I read slowly. Maybe I have slow eyes, I don't know. When I was younger I even took a speed-reading course. It was terrible. The technique they were teaching didn't work on me. I quit after two sessions. I watch people who breeze through a heavy text at lightning speed with the envy that some reserve only for the wealthy.

Because I read slowly, I savor every word, every phrase. I have no time or patience with bad writing or bad ideas. One would think that the slowness with which I digest books would put me off the habit, but it only increases my zeal. I chip away at massive tomes. I can't read for entertainment the way fast readers can. I save my guilty pleasures for other pursuits: sports, alcohol, rock'n'roll.

My attachment to books is sensual as well as intellectual. A friend of mine once broke my concentration to remark that I will caress a book as I read along. I hadn't noticed but it's true: my hands move constantly over the pages. I love to hold them, feel them. I love the way books smell. I will fold a paperback in two and break the spine. I will bend the spine of a hardback, feeling the turned page rend just enough until it rests loosely in position. Like a favorite old dog, the books I have read and loved hang around, sit in my lap, and keep me company. I pull volumes off my shelves that I have combed through a thousand times, their spines cracked, pages slipping from their moorings, and marked by underlines I have made. I'm fussy about those underlines and insist on using a sturdy straight-edged bookmark as an underlining ruler. I have a system of asterisks and paragraph side-lining. I scribble in the margins.

Old books, made on now-antiquated printing presses, have text you can run your fingers across, almost like braille, to feel the impressions left by the printer's art. I do appreciate a good book cover, too, and have shamelessly purchased many a volume for just that reason. But what I crave most is the liberating compensation of such a sublime labor: reading and learning from what I read. Every time I finish a book, I can honestly say I look up from that last page a different man.

On my last day of college, I was marching across campus after a particularly unpleasant row with a teacher over a grade, on my way into a process I had visited again and again—the meeting with my advisor, then the deputy department head, then the department head, then someone from the dean's office, to redress my grievance. Suddenly, the wind left my sails, and I stopped in my tracks. It was a brisk sunlit spring morning, the buds on the trees a delicious baby green. Dawn moisture had yet to burn away. Standing there on the pavement between buildings like a rock in a river, students hurrying in both directions in waves around me, I looked down at the books I was carrying. The one on top, which consumed all my attention, was something I was reading for my own edification, required by none of the courses I was taking. And I thought to myself, who are you kidding? Why argue again and again with these people? Are you ever going to win? Can you even survive in this environment? They have their agenda, you have yours. You could walk off this campus right now, go somewhere pleasant, and finish this marvelous book in peace.

And that's exactly what I did. But first, I went down to the campus bookstore and perused the shelves, not as a frantic student looking to fill his course load, but as a book lover, searching for titles of pure interest, in a book mart like no other, a college bookstore. I loaded up on psychology, politics, history, novels, essays, poetry, and then I left. I told myself I would never be back, I was through with college, through with school. My love of learning was real, and without the shackles of the education system to hold me back there would be no limits to my investigations. I was out of there. But I'll be goddamned if college has ever been through with me.

The Association of Writers & Writing Programs is an innocuous name for an organization of great literary minds. The AWP sponsors a conference held once a year, somewhere in North America, ostensibly for those who work in writing programs primarily at colleges and universities. Technically speaking, a "writing program" is a graduate-level program of instruction which results in a master of fine arts degree in poetry, fiction, or creative nonfiction. The AWP was begun by some ambitious educators at George Mason University in northern Virginia in 1967 who, proud of their own writing program, wanted to link up with other such programs to see what could be accomplished on a larger scale. Forty years later, there are four hundred participating schools, ninety-five nonacademic learning centers, and tens of thousands of writers affiliated in some way with their programs.

My first AWP conference took place in Vancouver, British Columbia. I had always wanted to visit Vancouver, a place about which I have never heard a negative thing. Plus, it was the year the National Hockey League suspended play to straighten out a labor dispute, and, being starved for my favorite sport, I heard that Vancouver had a really good minor league team called the Giants that would be entering the playoffs at the same time the conference was being held. So, for me, going three thousand miles for a writers' conference just made sense.

My wife would be attending and participating in two panels, one on the books of Howard Norman, and another on independent nonacademic writing programs such as The Writer's Center in Bethesda, Maryland, provide. Our plan was to arrive in town a few days early, stay someplace nice and romantic, get the lay of the land, and do some touristy stuff before hunkering down at the convention. It was a good plan. The only flaw in the plan was that I asked a Canadian buddy of mine who had lived and worked in Vancouver for several years where to go and what to see. We spent those first few precious days in an empty hotel by a deserted seaside that wasn't going to spring to life for another six weeks. Gray sky backed with gray cement. Thanks, Charley. So much for Vancouver.

The convention was held in a giant old world hotel called the Fairmont, in the heart of downtown. We had stayed at Fairmont hotels before, and my wife, ever doing research, had signed us up for a brownie points program that gives upgrades and cheaper rooms the more you stay with them. So even though we registered too late to get the conference rate, we found ourselves upgraded to an exclusive businesspersons' floor with office accomodations, daily shoeshine, laundry, and dry-cleaning service, and mercy of mercies, a decently stocked help-yourself bar. Peace, privacy, and free booze. So this is how the other half lives! Not bad for a couple of writers huckstering their work: one writing poetic retellings of ancient myths, and the other ranting and raving at the kakistocracy.

So when I wasn't sampling a tasty Scotch in the hushed privacy of our upstairs domain, where other conventioneers were not allowed, and feeling so very *elite*, I might add, I was haunting the cavernous and ornately detailed lobby lounge, oiling up the old harangue, and preying upon the tender souls of North American Academe. How oddly perfect that, instead of boring boisterous businessmen, with their pinched vocabularies and haughty arrogances, there were platoons of turtlenecks, blue jeans and sport coats—yes, some even with leather patches over the elbows—and billowing gypsy skirts or tight little sensible suits. These are people who drink wine and count their change, who quiver with naughty conspiratorial glee at the suggestion of having more than two glasses at a sitting. These are quiet people, reading or scribbling, or calmly and earnestly going about their conversations. Some are fretting over essays to be presented at panels before the most discerning audiences possible; some are vetting after having just done so. The more time you spend in this atmosphere, the more you realize how missing it is in the world outside these walls. These are people who live and thrive on research. To them it is fun. They don't watch television, except when something "quite good" is on. And although many are Luddites to whom the computer is an unwieldy and frustrating scourge, for most, the dawn of the Age of Process has made their professional lives so immensely easier, those joys of discovery have taken to soaring higher than ever. As they rethink their own processes, they find it a greater joy to teach, and share in the experience with others.

My wife's panel, for which she and the four other panel members had been preparing for weeks, went smoothly. She was talking about the use of a photograph as metaphor in Howard Norman's novel, *The Haunting of L.* Norman himself slipped into the room, furtive-like, as though he might be entering a trap, as if perhaps one of these scholars had detected a flaw in his craft. He was accompanied by legendary poet, teacher, and essayist Stanley Plumly and the keynote speaker from the night before, Canadian writer Alistair MacLeod.

MacLeod had delivered his address after tipping back quite a few beverages, it seemed. He had decided to get up in front of a largely American throng and give them all a long, doddering, pixilated discourse on the history and development of Canadian literature. The audience, peppered with earnest intellectuals and snappy, impatient agents from New York, Seattle, Chicago, and LA, was restless and condescending. But I loved it. I sought out the commercial-press bookstore the next morning and bought every title of his they had. He is a delight to read, with great depth of descriptive feeling about wilderness towns and life in the woods and lakes of the North. His prose is clean, bold, and unafraid, like the waters, forests, men, women, and beasts that populate his stories. Everyone I met said I was crazy to think what he did was cool. Everyone there was professional, on the best stage they have to display their work, and like true North Americans, they expect to be sold to, they want the pitch, and they want it delivered well. That's not what McCleod was all about. So be it.

Some of the attendees at the AWP have taken on mythological status with the rank and file. Certain names are whispered with reverence or unexpected joy. Mark Doty, Linda Gregerson, Galway Kinnell—these are literary minds of first rank who should be leading the discourse of the nation, but they are not. They dwell in the minor offshoot presses or independent presses. You can get their books, but you won't happen upon them. They might distract us from our real mission in life which, as we've been told again and again, is eating fast food, watching television, and letting others do our thinking and voting for us. "Americans watch six hours of television a day," Gore Vidal once said. "How can they defend their liberties when they're busy watching *The Gong Show*?" Insert *American Idol*, and I think you see his point. But we need to know what we are missing.

On the plane over, in honor of Hunter S. Thompson, who had recently killed himself, I was reading *Fear and Loathing: On the Campaign Trail '72*, which, by the way, is still as fresh, bold, and death-defying as when it was written. A book like that can spike one's testosterone or estrogen level, up the ante on one's refusal to compromise, remind one that the truth, plainly spoken, is a devastating thing to hear. We are all so starved for it these days; we look furtively about when we hear it, feeling suddenly naked in public. That's what it's like listening to these people make their witness, before packed committee meeting rooms normally reserved for hedge-fund operators and corporate movers of popular brands of toothpaste. Listening to Plumly, or Michael Ondaatje, Henry Taylor, or Coleman Barks—and now I'm picking names at random who have passed through the AWP or its overlapping parallel organizations—gets one's dander up at the shutting down of the American intellectual mainstream. It's a shameful reminder of how pitifully low the bar has been reset, and reminds one of all the noise and vulgarity we are subjected to every day in place of such heady and necessary discourse.

After the Howard Norman panel, David Swerdlow, a poet and professor from Westminster College, in Pennsylvania, was heard to lament, "If a panel for Howard Norman, why not one for Stan?" The wife and other panel members took up the call, and, by the end of the conference, plans were being made to honor Plumly with a panel on his work at the next AWP conference in Austin, Texas, the following year. Plumly is a leathery old coot who still has all his hair. He has a maverick's swagger and a youthful twinkle in his eye. The legion of individuals who have gone forth from his classrooms bent on writing well and forever is most impressive, almost spooky. I meet them everywhere. I will tease him when we meet that all his former students, when they hear his name, suddenly turn cold and glassy-eyed and repeat verbatim in a droning lifeless monotone, "Stanley Plumly is the greatest teacher in the world. Stanley Plumly taught me everything I know. I would be nothing today without Stanley Plumly," and the old boy geezes himself into a coughing fit, as his middle-aged and twenty-something acolytes alike nod automatically in agreement. Why his book of criticism, *Argument and Song,* is not required reading is a mystery. His publisher wouldn't even run a paperback edition.

I wasn't a good student. My home life growing up wasn't conducive to study or intellectual pursuits. In our house, if you were caught sitting reading a book you were accused of doing nothing. Wasting your time. That's just the way it was. The bathroom was the only safe place for reading. Dickens, Ian Fleming, Ray Bradbury, Herodotus, Steinbeck, Bierce, Orwell, Rod Serling, and countless Civil War and WWII historians and I spent a lot of time in the john together. I'm not complaining. I had a fascinating childhood full of adventure and wonder. And I wouldn't trade it. But I had to be careful not to let the vocabulary stretch out too ostentatiously around the house.

Also, the aging WWII generation didn't understand dissent. They took contradiction of authority as a personal insult, and they reacted accordingly. Thoreau to them was a filthy hippie, not a man of great intellectual courage. My father was a Depression Era Republican, mad as hell at "do-gooders" and liberals of any and all stripes, who found a savior in Barry Goldwater, and later Ronald Reagan. My mother was a Franklin Roosevelt/Pierre Trudeau liberal, and a Jack Kennedy Democrat. Things around my house could get loud and unpleasant.

It wasn't that my parents were unintelligent. They were very intelligent, but my mother thought the display of too much intellect phony or pretentious, and my father thought the only serious topic for conversation or concern centered around money. All else was bullshit, and he would tell you so. My mother read history and lots of it. Although she didn't complete high school, she must have had some readers among her family growing up, because she would quote Shaw, Voltaire, Franklin, Gibbon, and Jefferson all the time, without always knowing the source of her aphoristic wisdoms. People of that generation and those previous had those sayings on the tips of their tongues, sayings like "I don't agree with what you're saying, but I would defend to the death your right to say it," and "Youth is wasted on the young." The wisdom is what they drew their strength from, and those little quotations, like their prayers, were what they used to cope with a world of very few mercies. When did Americans stop memorizing and quoting their geniuses, or as my mother would put it in her old-world style, their betters?

As the 1960s gained momentum, parents of all houses noticed something terrible happening around the dinner table. Their kids were giving them contrary arguments to the conformist status quo, and were backing it up with the words of the intellectual masters, many of them American, from history. Young people were throwing what they perceived as their parents' shallow devotions back in their faces. It didn't set well. And as the political establishment became more and more right wing, the academic establishment was blamed for teaching this seditious rubbish in the first place.

This social dichotomy spilled over from the dinner table to the classroom. Teachers and administrators were just as divided as the rest of the country. Half of them wanted you to carry on a rigid social tradition and groom yourself accordingly—to go to Vietnam, if called, as they or their friends and loved ones had served in WWII and Korea. For them, supporting the government meant supporting your culture, your way of life—whatever that was. I remember after the famous first appearance of The Beatles on *The Ed Sullivan Show*, dozens of boys at my Catholic grade school showed up the next day with their hair combed down over their foreheads. They were sent home, suspended, and, in some cases, expelled. Later, at college, having a draft board office on campus was considered by many in authority a splendid idea. The draft office monitored grade-point averages of the male students who enjoyed a deferment if they kept their grades above a certain level, and scooped them up if they slipped below the line. Now this is where it got sick and twisted. Many professors would grade you down if they simply didn't like you, your style, who or what they thought you were. The military, they preached, would do you good. To counter that, other teachers, people of conscience, would try to lift you up, help you out with your grades, and shepherd you through the labyrinthine college administration. Both sides thereby created a totally adversarial and artificial environment. Not exactly the warm fuzzy place where you could curl up with Mr. Rabelais of an afternoon, but Mr. Nietzsche was always welcome.

Four years after I walked out of school, I was living in Georgetown, Washington, D.C., not far from the Georgetown University campus. I would stroll across campus like I owned the place, volunteer at the alternative rock radio station, scan the courses offered, and attend classes without ever applying or paying a dime. I was a phantom, losing myself in the throng of earnest faces, in the crush of preprofessional wannabees, future yuppies, young kakistocrats. If a professor looked out across his youthful charges and wrinkled his brow at seeing me nestled in the back of the class, when he looked again I would be gone. I took courses by Father Richard McSorely, who had been a prisoner of the Japanese for four years during WWII, was part of the radical Berrigan Brothers clan, and taught classes on the history of nonviolent activism. I took courses on Middle Eastern politics, civilian space exploration, the future of ground transportation, intelligence gathering, ethics, and literature. I even handed in final papers and, when I did, I signed them John Glenn, after the first American to orbit the Earth. School, I found out, can be a marvelous place if grades don't matter, if you never have to deal with its administration, if all you want to do is learn.

The Nixon/Reagan/Bush crowd blamed the liberal arts schools for dissention against the war in Vietnam. And they blamed their failure in that struggle on that dissension. Theirs was a dystopian universe where learning the very principles of the founding of America and holding the establishment to those ideals was in and of itself seditious. The right-wing militarists still believe that liberal dissent is why their policies failed. The Second Iraq War proved that wrong. There was no meaningful intellectual dissent against the Iraq War that would register on the average American's radar in the early/mid-2000s because by the time that conflict was engaged, the Arms Industry had partnered with big oil and computer conglomerates to buy up all the major communication industries, leaving those few independent voices small and insignificant and easily shouted down. By 2007, ninety-one percent of all talk radio was right-wing. The media at large was now definitely right-wing, pro-war, and anti-intellectual. No, the government botched the Iraq War up all by themselves. Protest from the left had nothing to do with it. Nevertheless, after Vietnam, "Liberal" Arts took a beating.

The bourgeois tuition-paying businessperson thinks all learning institutions should be glorified trade schools. If you aren't learning how to redesign his or her favorite widget, or become a useful bean counter, you're wasting your time, and ultimately, his or her money. Being proudly obtuse, the conservative minority boastfully excoriated anything with the "L" word in it, unaware that they pledge allegiance to what is technically a "liberal" democracy. They then set about destroying the liberal arts schools in America by transforming them into business schools. They also stripped the K–12 grades of so much funding, those who could afford it were forced to send their children to private schools, most of which are religion-based. And now they learn the hard way that a Liberal Arts major can do something that most business majors can't—i.e., write a cogent letter, analyze information, make an informed decision. Ask any corporate executive what he thinks of each year's batch of new recruits, and he or she will tell you all he hopes for is someone trainable. Memo to business school majors: Don't spend more than you take in—now go get yourself a life.

I know all this because your Reluctant Scholar toured American campuses as a musician during the 1980s and 1990s, playing to hundreds of schools a year. Our act involved political humor, and it was shocking to witness campus after campus go through a transformation from Liberal Arts to business right before our eyes. One semester, we would visit a campus that was famous for turning out intelligent history, English, and arts majors; the next semester we would return and find the campus bookstores jammed with accounting, statistics, and computer manuals.

On one tour through the State University of New York school system, we were awakened four nights in a row, at four different campuses, in the middle of the night, because some-one had pulled the fire alarm. As the dorms emptied and the bleary-eyed students scrambled out into the cold night air, we discovered it wasn't the fire department that went and checked out the buildings, but the local police, searching the students' rooms for evidence of alcohol. Students found with a single can of beer, empty or full, in their rooms, were summarily expelled. The fourth night it happened, a fireman explained to me that it was the police who had in fact pulled the alarms; the fire department only showed up because the law requires it when an alarm is pulled.

The following semester, we returned to play those cam-puses again. When I asked administrators how their evil pogrom was working out, they replied that they had to cancel the program because, in the midst of the Reagan-Bush Recession, they simply couldn't afford to lose all those tuitions.

As far as I was concerned, raising the drinking age from eighteen to twenty-one had little or nothing to do with public safety, and everything to do with the Freedom of Assembly. The rathskeller at the average big university could hold a thousand or fifteen hundred students. They were all shut down as the new law was grandfathered in. I simply don't believe that the government of that time gave a rat's ass about traffic fatalities or the safety and well-being of the youth of the country. It's about beefing up security, curbing dissent; it's about budgets and finding ways to keep them growing. And it was about preparing the youth of the country for a war in Nicaragua.

I will maintain till the bitter end that preventing a big war in Central America in the 1980s was the crowning achievement of the Peace Movement begun twenty-five years earlier.

◈

Meanwhile, back at the AWP, Marybeth Holleman, Linda McCarriston, and Richard Hoffman are giving a panel on what motivates writers, and issuing a basketful of encouragements for would-be authors to add heart and substance, to give three dimensions to their students' prosaic musings.

Holleman spoke about the Renaissance person being someone who prided himself or herself on being an "intellectual generalist," and how in our age of specialization, it is nigh-on impossible, even for academics, to break through the categorization mentality of corporate marketing theory when crafting a piece for publication. British philospher John Ralston Saul has even gone so far as to call the contemporary specialist "illiterate" once he or she steps outside his or her respective field, and he has a valid point.

Linda McCarriston continued in this vein, expressing a fear that in our current intellectual void capitalism has nothing left to dialogue with. She said that capitalism's other half is socialism, and the two concepts need each other to balance out society. But now, she lamented, capitalism ignores its spouse, socialism, and without its better half, talks down to its children—us.

By the time Richard Hoffman took the podium, we were softened up pretty good. Hoffman teaches memoir writing, and he starts his students out with the simplest question: "What is the conversation you were born into?"

Ask that question of the person sitting next to you, or of the author of the book laying in your lap. I was born smack dab in the middle of the Twentieth Century in the Capital of the Empire. Eisenhower, the McCarthy era, Beatniks, Marilyn Monroe, the Cold War, the Bomb. I was a patrol boy one Friday afternoon; we had been let out of school early without being told why. A voice from a passing car called out to me, "President Kennedy is dead!" I was eleven years old.

Three months later, The Beatles hit town.

Of course, one could ask Hoffman's question of a culture or a country. What was the conversation America was born into? Poet Rose Solari says that "If we (in the United States) are to have a literary tradition that can stand alongside older cultures, then we have got to claim our founding geniuses." I would add that those ideas, left behind by the great thinkers, are the very ideas that can save a culture when it flounders or suffers crises of spirit. Because the military draft was a genuine plague upon the youth of the nation, plucking young people from their classrooms, homes, and jobs, students wanted and needed the eloquence of the Founders, the Transcendentalists, the Reformers, to use as weapons of defiance. We turned to Walden Pond, a hundred and thirty years previous, and found, among others, a scruffy man who lived in a wood.

These days, freethinkers and intellectuals are on the run, besieged by what I would call the illiterati. America is a nation of merchants, and our culture has been defined by the merchant's aesthetic for so long, even members of the nonmerchant classes have learned to think in terms of extolling the virtues of an idea's earning power as part of its validation.

John Adams, America's first conservative president, once famously remarked that "I study war, so that my son will study business, so that his son will study art." And although businesspeople play a key role in the health of society, their cultural, intellectual, and philosophical contributions are by definition always narrow and limited—too narrow and limited to be allowed to take a leadership role in the culture of our society. They have usurped from academics and the philosophers around us, who, quite simply, have been shouted down and locked out of our governing and cultural processes by these same moneyed interests. It's as though Adams's son, the businessman, kept Adams's grandson, the artist, locked up and hidden somewhere on the estate, but every once in a while the little bastard, to everyone's chagrin, gets loose and runs free!

◈

Book-haters, people who make fun of ballet and classical music, or ridicule people who use words longer than three syllables, are dangerous dumb animals as far as I'm concerned. My compassion and tolerance for them is about as deep and profound as theirs is for me. People who are stupid by choice deserve to be laughed at, ridiculed, and shamed into admitting their shortcomings, not lionized for being "real," or somehow "genuine," or anything "noble." There is nothing noble about being stupid. Being ignorant—and proud of it—might make for soothing television drama, or a chest-beating seminar for jingoist op-ed writers, but it's a devastating sociopolitical illusion that those who know better have an obligation to dispel.

Now, in the first decades of the twenty-first century, educators have moved from anger and denial to acceptance. They are having to admit the failings of their own system, no matter the source of those failings, and put reading courses into their curriculums so that students are capable of advancement. And the students are eating it up. Nowhere is this more evident than at nonacademic learning centers, the best of which, in my very biased opinion, is The Writer's Center in Bethesda, Maryland. Whenever they post a class in reading good books, plays, or poetry, it fills up instantly with otherwise educated professionals—people smart enough to know they've been denied, and that their popular culture has moved away from substantive discourse. At the AWP I heard it everywhere, in the conference rooms, down the corridors, in the bars. All are having great success offering classes in the basics of reading, comprehension, and, ultimately, encouraging their students to write. It is a giant step backward from the culture of our parents, but it is a necessary step forward if we are to save our society, our culture, our democracy.

Listening in on the panel discussions, lingering in the lounge, strolling the halls and exhibit hall, I tried not to think of the fate these gentle people and their counterparts in history receive at the hands of brutal regimes. When, I asked myself, will intellectuals band together and fight anti-intellectualism? At what point will they have had enough of the right-wing religious fanatics, and take them on by going past them to their constituencies? When, if ever, will there be an intellectual movement that is combative in its lionization of the mind?

If intellectuals don't see the danger they've courted by allowing themselves to be herded into smaller and smaller communities, they will fall victim to the repetition of the very histories they teach in their classrooms: the book burnings, executions, censorship, and destruction many have seen with their own eyes. But although I rant and rave that these people need to train their considerable mental might at the hounds of idiocy who would defame and ridicule their work, I have to remind myself that these people aren't warriors, they are think-ers; they aren't killers, they're poets. Can thinkers become warriors? Sure they can. Should they be warriors? Not in a perfect world, but perhaps in this imperfect one, yes—but warriors of the mind. I think they've got the message. Everywhere I turned at the AWP, I saw educators, writers, and professional articulators standing their ground. These days they are even willing to take you by the hand, sit you down, and teach you how to read, rather than expecting you to already know.

The conversation I was born into is a mad harangue. And that's what a democracy should inspire. From inside it's loud, scary, and weird. It is frustrating and infuriating because it feels so chaotic. But it isn't chaos, not real chaos. Just once a person would like things to turn out right and orderly, but if that's what you want, then fascism is for you. From outside a democracy looks weak and disorganized. Enemies have watched from without and misread what they see and hear, concluding that such discord is a sign of weakness. But it is a strength. As long as we argue long and loud and publicly, we are safe, from without *and* from within.

The only time I regretted walking off campus on that long-ago spring morning was more than a decade later, the morning after playing a concert at Kenyon College in Gambier, Ohio. I had gotten up early to go to the campus laundry, and as I started doing my clothes, a couple of students queried me about the content and structure of the songs they had heard us play the night before. They wanted to know the purpose of the rowdy progressive politics lurking in the lyrics. They wanted to know the process by which the lyrics, the music, and the message were all laced together; was the end result, which seemed to them a frenzy of abandonment and fun, simply a spontaneous entertainment? And how much of what they thought they heard did we intend for them to take away from the event? Ragged out, tired, and delighted someone had noticed, I gave a serious answer. "I can't imagine going through all we do to place ourselves in front of an audience to then not have anything to tell them. So certainly, we mean every word. But that's no reason it shouldn't be fun."

Later, I went to explore the campus bookstore, and found a coffee shop in the lobby. There were big cozy chairs scattered all around; the place was teeming with students on a Saturday morning, flopped in chairs, lying on cushions on the floor, all reading, writing, or quietly discussing. One wall of the coffee shop had a rack of books all written by professors who teach or had taught there. I grabbed one off the shelf, poured myself a java, and nestled into a corner and spent an hour drinking it all in. I never wanted to leave campus. And in a sense I never have. I just had to arrive here, on my own terms.

Don't Answer the Phone!

I 've stopped answering the telephone and so should you. Why? It came to me recently, clear as a bell. We're not *supposed* to answer the phone, that's why.

"He doesn't even hear it anymore," my wife says about me and the telephone, and it's true.

"I've been at Jim's house when the phone rings, nothing happens!" a friend of mine quips as he sips good whiskey after a delicious and satisfying home-cooked dinner at our place. The fire is blazing, drinks flow, the conversation is lively and convivial. Then, with timing as perfect as in a TV sitcom, the phone rings. Silence. It rings three more times until the voicemail robot answers it. "See?" he delivers his punch line. "Nothing happens!" and everyone shrieks with laughter.

Actually, I am quick to explain, something did happen. The phone rang. A robot at the phone company intercepted the call, my friend got to give me a good-natured hard time in front of everyone, and we never broke stride. I secretly suspected the caller to be one of these very same wisenheimers secretly hitting the auto-call-Jimmy button on the cell phone in his pocket. Fine with me. Let them have their fun.

Certainly, all those present that night will remember it the next time they call and I don't answer. As far as they are concerned, I will forever be sitting here, drinking, alone, sitting right by the phone, listening to it ring, knowing it's them, and deliberately not answering. And that hurts their feelings.

I think my friends secretly get it, however. We are together, having a wonderful time. If I'm not expecting a call important enough to break up the evening, why answer the bell? Is there some DNA code encrypted in our brains that commands us to respond just because a bell goes off? Or maybe we are the victims of conditioning, the kind of conditioning that starts with something as innocent as the bells that ring between periods at school. Those bells were put in place during the Industrial Revolution to train kids to be good factory workers. Now we are accustomed to being buzzed, dinged, belled, bullied, and beeped throughout the day—told to put on our seat belts or empty the dryer, informed that the microwave is done, the coffee is made, our lights are still on, and this wonderful piece of surrealist absurdity, the door is ajar.

My high school class of rowdy hippies actually petitioned the school to turn the bells off. We found them insulting. After all, we had been sitting staring at the damned clock throughout each period of the day. On the hour, we were going to get up and shove off to the next class, bells or no bells. So let us have no bells. I understand as soon as we graduated and were out of the administration's hair, they turned the damned things back on again and no one said boo.

I find myself wondering here if they still ring bells between classes at school. I have no idea. I could call some friends and ask, I suppose, but I don't care enough, really, to pick up the phone.

The telephone has evolved from an incredibly useful daily aid to an invasive and challenging adversary, a potential monster, really, that we can and must control if we are to have any peace or get anything done. How it got this way, I'm not sure. Somehow, when no one was looking, someone passed a law, took advantage of a good thing, or simply let the wrong people take over, and boom, the sanctity of the inner sanctum was gone. The corporateers had found a way in, under the door, through cracks in the infrastructure, through the telephone.

Maybe this new adversary was born when telemarketers gained access to my home phone, or when junk mail began to outnumber the personal and necessary correspondence that arrives at my domicile every day. Or maybe it was when commercials on TV became more entertaining than the programming meant to deliver them, thus rendering the TV completely useless once and for all, that I suddenly looked at the phone on the wall, or the one in my pocket, and thought, wait a minute! This is just another goddamned idiot box! And since when does every idiot get to ring my bell? And where does it say I'm obligated to respond?

My parent's generation believed that the phone was something precious, miraculous even, that should be used responsibly.

"People wouldn't call unless it was important," they would scold. Imagine. Now, people half my age and younger no longer even have a home phone. Why shoulder the expense? This group has no idea what it's like for the phone to ring without knowing who, as we used to say, is on the other end of the line. Imagine the horror.

"It's long distance!" children from my generation used to hear our parents exclaim. Long distance calls cost a lot of money. But back then, the caller was paying, not caller *and* callee. Sometimes it was difficult to get a connection. There was this great primitive hiss on the line that made the voices sound distant, so much so that people shouted to each other as if their voices could traverse a great abyss of space and time. Long after satellites and technology solved the audio and connection difficulties, those callers still kept screaming. Cell phones entered the scene with similar primitive glitches and idiosyncrasies. "Can you hear me now?"

In the Old Days, the average person had no idea how a voice could travel electronically. The operation of the telephone had some connection with the miracle of electricity: they both, the phone and electrical power, traveled through wires suspended on tree posts, wires that stretch from my house and around the whole world. That's a lot of wires. And here, the capacity of human beings to accept an abstraction as reality intersects with their capacity for common sense. I don't know how it works, but it does; therefore, other things/ideas that don't work yet might someday. In this way the telephone is linked to an innate human survival instinct, the curiosity to see what opportunities lie in the next unknown moment. We are curious because we hunger, we fight to survive, we need to breed. This survival strategy also makes us socially addicted gossips and rumor-mongers. No one is exempt. The ancient grapevine has evolved from hushed whispers in corridors and across fences to the telegraph, the telelphone, and on to the Internet, and back to the phone again. The human grapevine remains fascinating in its power, which is growing exponentially.

Not knowing who was on the other end of the line also injected a heightened sense of immediacy, excitement, and daring to a phone call. When the phone rang, it suddenly introduced the notion that everything in your life could change, for good or ill, if you just picked it up. Who could resist?

You're hired.

You're fired.

Yes, she'll go out with you.

Someone's getting married.

A friend is in love.

A friend is heartbroken.

Let's make plans.

Someone is dead.

Someone important, maybe Dear Aunt Agatha, would call long distance during the dinner hour, hoping to catch us all in at the same time. It wasn't an imposition; it was exciting. We'd take turns coming from the table to the phone and it was like having her there with us for supper. Each one would have a precious minute with her on the phone. And after she hung up, we would chatter happily away, like birds around the feeder, at all the news. The telephone was an instrument of the tribe, like the fire, the hearth, the dog, the car.

Well, anymore, Dear Aunt Agatha is dead, and it's the corporateers who are calling, and calling, and calling.

The telephone has become more than a symbol of our accessibility. The home number is our virtual address, and marks us on the map of the world. The phone is a gateway to our private lives. We enjoy the illusion of having some control over who knows how to find us, but we know that isn't true. Your home phone, if you have one, has replaced your social security number as an identifier. Turn on your cell and it's like Frodo putting on the magic ring. Somewhere far away a giant eye opens and it looks right at you.

Dick Tracy's wristwatch, dreamed up by comic book visionary Chester Gould, was a two-way phone/two-way TV/two-way computer. Gould foresaw the use of wiretapping and voice recognition, among other things. For my generation, it was watching Captain Kirk flip open his communicator that made the gadget geek in all of us say, "Hey, that's sweet! Give me one of those!"

But the Faustian joke on us all, certainly, is that we can't beam up, Scotty, not yet.

The cell phone has morphed into an elaborate toy for young people, and a crutch for businessmen and lovers. And cell phone etiquette is worse than land-line etiquette ever was. Admit it. How many times have you been waiting in line at a retail counter or at an airport when some businessman with a fragile ego starts calling his associates with the incredibly urgent information that he is, indeed, standing in a line? Or seen a woman babbling away on a cell phone while changing lanes in fast-moving traffic with a car full of kids? I do get a kick out of watching teenagers use their cell phones. It takes me back to a time when the outside world consisted mainly of friends, in league with one another against the absurdities of the straight responsible world all around us. Now they can publish their reactions to that world from their cell phones, and that becomes yet another object lesson in social interaction and its potential consequences.

Here, I must digress and vent a little about what I call Gadget Geeks. Sadly, they are mostly men. Recently I was at the cell phone store to replace a lost unit. It was one of those infuriating stores where there are plenty of cashier stations, but management has only one person on per shift to handle customers. In front of me in line was a fellow, roughly my age, a lost unit if ever I saw one, wearing a trendy belly pack, expensive jeans, and an outdoorsman's vest and boots. An urban mountain-man, I guess, come out of the suburban foothills and landed here in trendy upscale urban Bethesda, Maryland, with an I've-been-to-the-gym-four-times-a-week-physique. He was there for half an hour, and when the clerk finally screwed up the courage to ask this fellow if he wanted to buy anything, the answer was no, he was just getting caught up. I wanted to shoot them both with a high-powered super-soaker full of mountain moose piss! The Twenty-First Century will be a heaven for Gadget Geeks, I'm afraid—grown men addicted to video games, computer freaks wasting away into silly putty as they sit mesmerized before their screens.

There's also an element of infantalization about Gadget Geekness. On a Friday evening, my wife and I emerged from a movie to see a line of adults a hundred feet long waiting at the ice cream store next to the theater, while around the corner, the bar was almost empty. It was enough to make me want to cry. I haven't liked ice cream since I was twelve years old, and nearly every guy in line waiting for his ice cream treat was playing with his…cell phone.

What happens with most of us, I think, is that a novelty can be fun, but when novelty wears off, all we seek is a certain comfort level with our technological environment so we can settle down, burrow in, and get some work done. In my youth, I was the one people came to when their new stereo systems needed hooking up. But somewhere along the line, I quit keeping up with the latest thing and went on sort of a technological cruise control. A decent tape deck, a reliable typewriter, and some rabbit ears on my American-made Magnovox TV set were the staples of a happy and productive life. You may think, reading this, that I am an angry Luddite, or some grouchy turn-back-the-clock has-been. That may very well be, but I'll have you know that between my office phones, home office phone, home phone, and family, there are ten telephone lines and three cell phone accounts I'm responsible for. And I won't answer any of them.

You see, as I said earlier, we really aren't intended to actually answer the damn thing anymore. Think about it. The government doesn't answer the phone. Neither do the major corporations and damn near all the lesser ones. They don't want to talk to you. And why should they? Got a problem with our product? Throw it away and buy another one. Got a problem with your government? Too damn bad, you voted us in, or worse, you didn't even care enough to go to the polls. Your satisfaction, as far as they are concerned, was guaranteed the minute you passed the credit check. They don't have to answer the phone; you can't make them. Taking care of your bullshit problem has become the job of the website or the numerical selection recording. Sometimes they just come right out and tell you to get lost. "The Wizard sez, 'Go away!'"

Well, I am simply recommending you do the same thing.

The commonplace house phone is done, over, toast. And good riddance. It has outlived its usefulness. And the cell phone? Well, from now on we'll know who's calling and why. Pertinent facts and ideas can be passed along without the inconvenience of actual contact, and much faster. But by and large, bad manners and atrocious etiquette have become mainstays of public adult behavior, especially where the telephone is concerned, and my only conclusion is that, mercy of mercies, you can at least turn the damned thing off. And when I do, this will be my voicemail robot's response:

Hi, your call is being handled by the Cosmo Demonic Telephone Company, the same company that provides Mr. Patterson with telephone service. There will be a one dollar charge for handling your call over and above your regular phone service charge, a nuisance fee that will go directly to Jim. He thanks you for calling. Please choose one of the following options:

- If you have called to bawl me out for not answering the phone, press one.
- If you have called to bawl me out for another reason, press two.
- If you're a friend of mine in need of some money or assistance, get in line, oh, and press three.
- If you're a relative of mine, and have called because you think you get to pass on to me all the stress you've let accumulate in your poor tortured psyche and think I can handle it, I can't, get in another line, and press 4.
- If you're a telemarketer, televangelist, teleprompter, or telefuckinanythingelse, press this…
- If you called to simply tell me you love me, anyway and regardless, well, God Bless You…and press on.

Thanks for calling, and I promise to get back to you just as soon as I possibly can…find a good reason to.

Just don't call me.

I'll call you.

Well, maybe.

Something Out of Nothing

(a short story)

Freddy Robinson makes me sick.

Honestly, I just hate old men who wear their pajamas all day long. I tell him that if he had a shred of self-respect and dignity left, he would get up in the morning and get dressed like the rest of us. But no. Five minutes before Lois clears breakfast he comes shuffling in wearing the same old slippers, rumpled gray pajamas, a three-day growth, hair jutting out in all directions, a big vapid yellow-toothed grin, and the same disgusting red plaid bathrobe he had on when he said good night. I swear, some night when he's asleep I'm going to take that robe out in the street and burn it right in front of the house! He insists that my animosity stems from the fact that he routinely beats me at chess. He is wrong. When he mentions this he looks to the others for support, and they, inexplicably, nod their heads as if now they understand the real reason for this unpleasantness over his unseemly toilet. It is a fact that his constant mastery of my game is a source of never-ending torment to me. Much worse than the pain in my hip or the nagging worry over the numbness in my leg and the financial strain of keeping up my treatments. But it is the sight of him, his odious demeanor, and his obvious disdain for the sensibilities of others that annoys me to the point of distraction.

Barbara is the nurse I have hired to come in every afternoon and see that the house members are all in good shape. After losing Ida the way we did, it's a comfort to know there is someone nearby. It's rather like having a mechanic on duty, but better. I like large fannies and I have made it absolutely clear to her and to anyone else who might be interested that I hired her because of her big rear end. Anyone who doesn't like it can take their twelve hundred dollars a month and go die someplace else. Barbara has taken a liking to us and drops in from time to time when off duty. Sometimes she'll take one of us to the theater or to see a film or just out for a ride to enjoy a beautiful morning. Barbara's grandfather was in vaudeville; she grew up around show people, so we have something we can talk about. Barbara may have figured out that my Tuesday afternoon luncheons with my nephew Kevin are purely fictitious, but she has the common sense to keep that intelligence to herself. After my treatments, I always enjoy a couple of whiskeys at the Lodge. This gives a festive touch to the deception when I return.

We live in a Big Old House, which I bought at an estate sale many years ago. There is an extra bedroom that goes unrented that we use for a quiet room and library. Janelle spends most of her time there, as do I. Most people our age live in constant fear of nursing homes or old-age homes. We are fortunate to have this alternative. I let them think that their membership here is democratic. We take a vote, then, if things don't turn out the way we thought, well, changes are made. After all, it is my house and I am the one who will quietly handpick the people I choose to die with. Except for Freddy. I'm not sure how he got here. And although he is the one who is usually stirring up the others, who, for some unfathomable reason, seem terribly fond of him, he is easily anticipated and overruled.

The Big Old House also has a fabulous front porch where, during fine weather, most of us want to be. Gina invites friends to play cards. Freddy pretends to read but just sits there waiting for cars to go by. He scowls at the local kids with a truly ugly countenance. In that regard, he's better than a watchdog. Ed sits up in the evenings and listens to ball games on the radio. My favorite time of day is just before dawn when I can have the porch all to myself. I put on a collar and tie. Nice slacks and shoes. A sport coat. I step out onto the platform to the applause of crickets, the neighbor's cats, and the cars parked along the street. The street lamp across the way looks like a great white spot.

"Ladies and gentlemen:"

It always began with bright blue lights. Two of them, either side by side or set apart, were suspended at eye level in the darkness like two great blue suns set in space. But there was no vacuum there. Indeed, the space between me and the burning blue was filled with a churning and volatile consciousness.

A litter of protean forms, sheltered by the darkness. Hungry sentient carnivores, an unruly lot of boors and bourgeois who would, when emboldened by their numbers and presumed solidarity given their common investment of an evening and a theater ticket, react en masse to my trained and ready utterances.

"Yes folks, my mother was good to me. She always told me, son, never take candy from strangers...unless they offer you a ride. You can see I've been around the block a few times."

They were easily tamed. The advantage was mine. I had a secret weapon. I introduced them to Eva. She turned them into a gelatinous goo. They hadn't a chance. Their poor fragile undeveloped libidos lay helpless before her like plump ripe poppy blossoms before the scythe. God, there were times when I envied the poor bastards. She could give them a look and with the turn of a shapely leg and the raising of an eyebrow set them to squirming audibly in their seats, or smile a smile that none of them had seen since their mothers welcomed them home from their first day of school.

Eva was trained for the ballet but was too small and voluptuous, too adventurous for the respectable stage. A tragic blend of sex, talent, and wisdom, what a timid person might call worldly. Adrienne Lecouvreur was her hero. "Oh to be poisoned by love and to die in the arms of my sweet savant!" Once Eva was on stage, the rest of the company could relax.

Out front, the theater was always clean and orderly. There was paper in the bathrooms, the ticket-takers and ushers were polite and efficiently courteous. Backstage everything was broken, dirty, and chaotic. Nothing worked and no one cared. No one cared about you because you didn't care about them. Neither party could afford an emotional investment of that kind. When the show is over, we're going to push on and with any luck we'll never see the joint again. Everyone carries a heart broken in two places. One by love, and the other by the stage. Everyone has that in common. A cynical smile covered a knowing eye that in turn covered the last burning ember of hope one would never admit to but would protect with all the strength and guile that could be summoned. And one can summon vast reserves of cunning and guile. A strange bond formed. It was temporary and forever. Well, nothing is forever, I suppose.

"I'll sleep when I'm dead," Eva would trill as she waltzed off on the arm of some wealthy patron after a show. I wonder if she's sleeping now.

I booked the gigs and wrote the routines. I always left something extra in her envelope. She was terrible with money and couldn't hang onto men either. She would fall asleep with her head in my lap in the back of the bus and I would fan her with an old program. Her mouth, so sensuous when animated was, when at rest, a wound, a painful-looking flaw in the otherwise elegant perfection of her small, delicate face. She never loved me, I know, though she loved nearly everyone else. My flaws were too well hidden. She found self-confident and self-contented men a bore.

She did give me a chance one time. It was in some small town somewhere I've now forgotten. Far away. We had a rare night off between shows. The others all had colds and so took advantage of the layoff to stay in at the hotel. Eva had the idea that it would be a gas to dress up like normal people and go out to dinner like a normal couple and have normal conversation and eat normal food. I found a business suit in a costume

trunk, and she put on a soft cotton dress and a string of cheap
fake pearls with matching earrings. She arranged a curl in
front of each ear and parted her hair on the side, like a boy. All
night long she pretended to hang upon my every word. Her
usual ceaseless babble about art and theater and who's this and
who's that, which never concerned me and never allowed me
to get a word in edgewise, was strikingly absent from her conversation. She had a look of bemused concern upon her face
all evening. We made eye contact all night. In fact, as I remember it now, she must have revealed her whole sweet ironic life
to me in those flashes and flares. Alas, I was too young, too
harried, to interpret them with enough accuracy to be of any
help to her, I'm afraid.

When we left the local steakhouse and went to a local bar,
we were tipsy, in hysterics. Her arms draped around my shoulders as she whispered her impressions of the Plain Janes and
Johns from the restaurant in my ear, the two of us exploding
with laughter as we stumbled into the bar. Once inside she
resumed her act of being normal. We even exchanged dry,
familial kisses to authenticate our routine.

We kissed good night at her hotel room door. A long,
sweet, tongueless, thank you kiss, from the girl of my dreams
for the boy next door. She would mention that night from time
to time with a wry, happy smile. For a day or two, the others
eyed us suspiciously, on the chance that assuming something
had happened between us they might coax us into revealing if
something actually had. I was willing to let them believe what
they would, but things were moving pretty fast.

"When we get to New York I'm going to take my money
and buy a beautiful fur coat, seamless stockings, new heels,
and wear nothing else for an entire week!" When we got to

New York she disappeared forever. Didn't make opening night. In a panic to fill time, I dressed like a woman and did our old tango number all by myself, a fading beauty giving a last dance to a world that was passing her by, dancing with my own ghost, with tears streaming down my face as tears of laughter flowed freely from the crowd. It was a smash. It made me famous for a while. Eva sent me a telegram of congratulations, "Once again, as always, something out of nothing, hugs & kisses—Eva," leaving no return address. I repeated that horrific goodbye many times over the years. It was one of my most popular numbers.

The morning paper hits the porch just before intermission. I read the box scores and wait for Lois to arrive and fire up the kitchen. Today is the Fourth of July and the boys at the Lodge always throw a big parade. It's really just a big pain in the ass. I don't know why I even bother. It seems like every time someone needs an old fool for a community production or a Santa Claus or a eulogy, my card gets punched. They always say it's for the children. I suppose it is. Or rather, to get the children to even notice we exist. Freddy wants in so bad that every time the Lodge is mentioned he fidgets like a schoolboy who can't control his bladder. I tell him we don't admit cranky old fucks in their pajamas. This really pisses him off. If he was smart he'd let me win at chess a little more often.

I'll go up to the attic and open the trunk. Maybe I'll put on the big Indian headdress I used to wear during Eva's Pocahontas number. "Katchawiggawaggamogga?" Eva would ask the open-faced guys in the crowd, causing their tongues to fall out of their mouths. Yes. The headdress should do fine. Little Carol should like that. I'll ride atop the fire engine and wave to her. Oh yes, there's an air show too. She loves to watch airplanes. Now that I think of it, she probably won't even notice me.

Kids.

Shit.

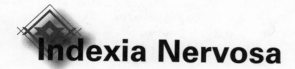

Indexia Nervosa

(a guide to the people and places who make up the territory of *Bermuda Shorts*, along with recurring themes and thought-forms, as well as geographies that exist solely within the author's mind)

Follow the further adventures of William Zachary Harper in the novel *Roughnecks* by James J. Patterson and Quinn O'Connell, Jr.